IN DEFENCE
OF ARISTOCRACY

IN DEFENCE
OF ARISTOCRACY

PEREGRINE WORSTHORNE

HarperCollins*Publishers*

HarperCollins*Publishers*
77–85 Fulham Palace Road,
Hammersmith, London W6 8JB

www.harpercollins.co.uk

Published by HarperCollins*Publishers* 2004
1 3 5 7 9 8 6 4 2

A catalogue record for this book
is available from the British Library

ISBN 0-00-718315-1

Set in Galliard by
Rowland Phototypesetting Ltd,
Bury St Edmunds, Suffolk

Printed and bound in Great Britain by
Clays Limited, St Ives plc

CONTENTS

Acknowledgements   vii

Prologue   1

One   9

Two   54

Three   93

Four   109

Five   168

Epilogue   214

I love it [aristocracy], like history.

Sylvia Plath

The hereditary permanency of families, and sets of families . . . are an invisible social asset on which every kind of culture is more or less dependent.

Labordere, quoted in Robert Skidelsky,
John Maynard Keynes

Acknowledgements

I want to acknowledge the great debt I owe to Larry Siedentop's fine essay on De Tocqueville (Oxford University Press, 1994) and his learned and lively *Democracy in Europe*, every page of which only served to confirm me in my belief that without an aristocratic dimension that noble ideal can never be realised. Siedentop himself, it needs to be said, reaches no such conclusion. Aristocracy is dismissed as a thing of the past. But it is often an embarrassing mark of a great work, such as his, to have *unintended* consequences.

I also want to thank Professor Vernon Bogdanor, of Brasenose College, Oxford, Edward Skidelsky and Derwent May for their very great kindness in reading my book and making invaluable suggestions. In no way, however, should their kindness allow them to be saddled with any responsibility for my conclusions.

And most important of all I want to pay tribute to my secretary, Claire Allan, whose patience, mastery of the computer, wise advice and encouragement have smoothed my path at every turn. The librarians at the London Library, too, have been unfailingly helpful, well beyond the call of duty.

Thanks are also due to Caroline Michel and Michael Fishwick, of Harper Collins, for not being put off by an unfashionable theme, and to Catherine Heaney and Kate Hyde for so cheerfully and efficiently getting the book into print.

And apologies to my wife for any embarrassment caused.

Prologue

Not only does every country have the aristocracy it deserves, but so does every era, including the democratic era. In this essay the term is used in two senses: first, to describe families whose power and authority, high prestige and assured dignity, depended upon titles of nobility dating back, in some cases, to feudal times; and, second, to describe families whose power and authority depend not so much on the distinction of ancient lineage as on what the distinguished American historian John Lukacs* calls 'distinctions derived from the consanguinity of their families with high civic reputation'; in other words, on a record of public service rather than on blood. Of the first it could be said that they were powerful and authoritative because they were noble; of the second that they were noble because they were powerful and influential.

Mr Lukacs suggests that a better term to describe this second meaning – families who are noble because they are powerful and influential, rather than the other way around – would be 'patrician' rather than aristocratic. They have something in common he writes, 'with the old patrician

---

* John Lukacs, *Philadelphia: Patricians and Philistines, 1900–1950* (New York: Farrar, Straus and Giroux, 1981).

societies of modern Europe, nearer to the middle of the continent, with a social and civic order incarnated by the great merchant families in cities such as Basel, Geneva, Amsterdam, Hamburg, or with the *grand bourgeois* (often Protestant) families in France . . . little in common with Proust's world of the Guermantes; many things in common with the world of Buddenbrooks (which Thomas Mann described in 1901) . . . solidly bourgeois (in the best sense of that often used word) and not glitteringly feudal.' Mr Lukacs's point is well taken. In the nineteenth and twentieth centuries, the description 'patrician' catches the flavour of the English ruling class rather better than the word 'aristocratic', covering, as it does, both Peel and Salisbury, Disraeli and Gladstone, Harold Macmillan and Hugh Gaitskell, even, just, both Tony Blair and Michael Howard. Nevertheless, out of habit, I have decided to stick to aristocratic and aristocracy and to leave it to the reader to make the necessary adjustment according to the context.

In any case, central to both meanings is the idea of certain families, joined together by the invisible bonds of memory, as bearers of important moral and social values and political traditions that carry authority because they have been demonstrated, to the satisfaction of all classes, to have served the public interest over many generations.

An aristocracy must also have another intangible source of power and authority – transcending all the others – that comes from longevity; from having been around long enough to have become an integral part of the nation's history and mythology. So without that time-honoured place in a nation's history and mythology an aristocracy ceases to be an aristocracy, and reverts back to being an ordinary power elite, whether in the form of plutocracy, oligarchy, a military junta, or meritocracy. In other words, the authority of an aristocracy, like that of a theocracy, depends on the power of faith: the public's faith in it and the aristocracy's faith in itself. It profits an aristocracy little, therefore, to retain only its wealth and power because without that intangible element of faith – beyond the range of political scientists to identify or quantify – it is no more than sounding brass and tinkling cymbals.

In this essay I shall try to argue that because of the British aristocracy's uniquely successful past, residual elements of the old faith still survive, along with even larger elements of its old wealth and influence. Legal status is also a factor. At the time of writing, the aristocracy still has legal status. Titles are officially bestowed and recognized, and a certain number of hereditary peers are still allowed to take a seat in the House of Lords, albeit only if elected by their fellow peers. But legal status could be more of a liability than an asset because, as John Stuart Mill famously remarked, 'the best way to discredit an idea is to give it a privileged, legal status'.

Unquestionably this causes resentment, and in some ways, therefore, the French, who got rid of the privileged status of their aristocracy in the eighteenth century by cutting off their heads, and the Americans, who never had such an aristocracy in the first place, are now less upset by the idea of aristocracy than the British. So much is readily admitted in this essay. In today's climate a *de jure* privileged aristocracy with titles of nobility and places in parliament may be an enemy of *de facto* hereditary aristocracy, which merges so imperceptibly into the ranks of meritocracy as not to present any visible target on which doctrinal egalitarians can train their guns. So it could well be that the idea of aristocracy in Britain would be strengthened rather than weakened by the removal of their legal privileges.

In any case, as this essay also tries to show, the role of the hereditary aristocracy in British history was so massive and splendid that it cannot – much as it might like to – just fold up its tents and fade away. The public and media won't let it. It is still too much part of 'us'; too deeply embedded in the nation's literature and culture; indeed in the national consciousness itself. What is more, its code of gentlemanly behaviour, which was eventually adopted by substantial elements in all classes, came to enjoy the status of a sub-Christian cult, exercising on many (for whom the demands of Christianity were too arduous) a more direct influence for good than did Christianity proper. So although in theory it might be wonderful to replace aristocratic deference with civic republicanism, that is most unlikely to happen in the foreseeable future. What is much more likely to happen – indeed is already happening – is the replacement of aristocratic deference, not by civic republican pride, but by something much more like egalitarian hypocrisy at the top and proletarian rancour at the bottom.

Plainly, therefore, some opening of minds is needed. Reactionary supporters of the class system, if there are any left, must understand how offensive it is to contemporary public opinion for the State to reserve positions of power and influence at the top of society – in the House of Lords, for example – for men and women whose individual talents would not otherwise justify them holding these positions. Most anti-egalitarians, I would imagine, have now conceded this point. But most egalitarians, unfortunately, are still as far as ever from opening their minds to the no less important truth that for the power of the State to be used to create a wholly classless society is equally objectionable. By a classless society* they presumably mean one in which those running things in the present have no association with those who ran them in the past; in which those running things are all drawn from families who have not themselves been running things; a society, that is, in which the only social distinction officially approved of is the one separating the minority that is running things (i.e. the elites) from the majority who are not running things (i.e. the masses). While such a society would certainly do away with individuals enjoying positions at the top of society to which their inherent talents do not qualify them – a marginally desirable development – it would also mean that the social space at the top occupied by those who deserved to be at the top would be demoralizingly barren and thin – a fundamentally undesirable

---

* T. S. Eliot, *Notes Towards the Definition of Culture* (Faber & Faber, 1948).

development. A state-sponsored classless society would be an atomized society. It doesn't bear thinking about. In other words, there *ought* always to be a social space at the top of society in which vestiges of the past (elites emeritus, so to speak) remain. Otherwise life at the top will be horribly nasty, brutish, and short, with grim consequences for life at every other social level.

In the past the State has smiled on aristocracy, and in this essay I lovingly adumbrate the benefits this country over the centuries has garnered from an aristocracy so favoured. But I also recognize that smiling on aristocracy, in the present climate, is no longer acceptable. To that degree, egalitarianism must rule. But only to that degree. What must not happen is that the smile should be replaced by a frown; that legal discrimination in favour should be replaced by legal discrimination against. In short, what this essay seeks to help create is a state of public opinion in which the old upper classes and their institutions, shorn of their legal privileges, are once again seen as a source of strength rather than weakness; a blessing rather than a curse; and above all, as ideally suited – rather than exceptionally unsuited – for public service.[*]

So this essay is not just a lament for the passing away of aristocracy; it is quite as much a plea for it to be given a new and constructive lease of life. For the only way to

---

[*] It is ludicrous, for example, that a 'toff' should be excluded from becoming leader of the Conservative Party; almost as ludicrous as a Catholic not being allowed to become Pope.

supersede an aristocracy that has done such historic service as Britain's has is to incorporate it. Only by continuing to use it, can we go beyond it.*

---

* José Ortega y Gasset, *The Revolt of the Masses* (1932).

One

Others ascribe to me alternately democratic or aristo-cratic prejudices; perhaps I might have had one or the other if I had been born in another century and in another country. But as it happened, my birth made it very easy for me to guard against both. I came into the world at the end of a long revolution which, after having destroyed the old order, created nothing that could last. When I began my life, aristocracy was already dead, and democracy was still unborn. Therefore, my instincts could not lead me blindly towards one or the other. I have lived in a country which for forty years has tried a little of everything and settled nothing definitively. It was not easy for me, therefore, to have any political illusions ... I had no natural hatred or jealousy of the aristocracy and, since that aristocracy had been destroyed, I had no natural affection for it, for one can only be strongly attached to the living. I was near enough to know it intimately, and far enough to judge it dispassionately. I may say as much for the democratic elements. ... In a word, I was so nicely balanced between the past and the future that I did not feel instinctively drawn toward the one or the other. It required no great effort to contemplate quietly both sides.

Alexis de Tocqueville

The spark that fired me into writing this essay on the impor-tance of the class system to English democracy was the following paragraph in Richard Hoggart's final volume of memoirs, *First and Last Things*:

> Democracy is never an abstraction. It has to be rooted in a sense of our own particular culture, of its virtues, strengths, limitations ... It arises from the people we have known, loved, respected as we grew up, whether that was among the urban or rural working class, or the conscientious and public-spirited among the middle class, or the upper class.

'*Or the upper class*'. Those were the four words that did the trick. For although I knew Mr Hoggart to be a most fair-minded man, I could not stifle the suspicion that he had added them only in a spirit of giving the devil his due – rather as a child feels obliged to add the name of some much disliked gorgon of an aunt to its bedtime supplications. Could he sincerely have believed, I asked myself, that a member of the British upper class had anything useful to contribute on the subject of British *democracy* except in an apologetic, exculpatory, or at best nostalgic mode? And if Mr Hoggart did so believe, surely he should at least have warned such a person to keep quiet about his own aristocratic provenance, lest readers should dismiss his views as likely to be self-serving and anachronistic, harking back to the 'good old days' when everybody knew where they stood but only a privileged few, like himself, enjoyed being there?

But then I had second thoughts. Why on earth should not a member – which I myself in part am – of the very class that, in 1688, created England's particular kind of democracy, and presided over its glorious destiny for over three hundred years, have something useful to say about its future? True, such a person, with roots in the upper-class culture, would be less qualified than Mr Hoggart, with his roots in the working class, to write about the 'virtues, strength, limitations' of English democracy from the bottom-dog perspective of the ruled; but did not that suggest, by the same token, that he would be more qualified to write about them from the equally if not more important top-dog perspective of the rulers?

Democratic top dogs? Is that not a contradiction in terms? Most emphatically not, since this is precisely what English aristocrats were: an organic part of England's democratic body politic, no more or less an organic part of that body than were the bottom dogs. Was not Winston Churchill, grandson of a Duke, but elected by the people, also, in the English sense, a democrat – someone, like Brutus, prepared to take up arms against tyranny? In England love of freedom, not a lack of quarterings, was and is the true test. Trying to write the aristocratic dimension out of English democracy, therefore, is like trying to write the Prince of Denmark out of *Hamlet*.

In my youth, of course, they tended to try to do the opposite: to write the working class out of the story. England's democracy seemed then to consist exclusively of grandees, most with titles. It was a view of democracy from the top downwards. Now, however, the fashionable view is increasingly from the bottom upwards. Thus the success or failure of England's democracy, which in the old days was largely measured by the statesmanship of its leaders and the standing of the country, is now largely measured by the quality of the man in the street.

In this essay, mindful of Mao's dictum about the fish rotting from the head downwards, I try to redress the balance, not, I hasten to say, so as to advocate reinstating the upper class – or anything as absurdly reactionary as that – but so as to highlight the gaping hole left in the head of our body politic by its extinction; its extinction, moreover, without any serious thought having been given to how, and with whom, that great empty hole should be filled. From time to time newspaper commentators amuse us by pretending that 'Tony's cronies' have filled the hole. That only shows how little the role of the old ruling class, in the sense that it is used in this essay, is understood.

The difficulty here, I believe, is that ever since the problems created by the Industrial Revolution, political and social thinkers in Britain, as in the rest of the world, have been concerned exclusively with the condition of the tail – the poor and the underprivileged. And quite rightly so since, thanks to the Victorian reforms of the public schools, of Oxbridge, and of the Civil Service, the elites, by the end of the nineteenth century, were in pretty good shape. What so much more obviously and urgently needed attention was the quality of life, moral and material, not of the few but of the many.

Roughly speaking, that still remains the state of play today. While there have been endless studies of the demoralizing effects of inner-city living conditions, or of capitalism generally, on the poor and underprivileged, there have been none, so far as I know, of the demoralizing effects of gross suburban affluence in such towns as Beaconsfield and Gerrards Cross – where there is a Mercedes and/or a BMW in every garage – and of capitalism generally on the rich and overprivileged.* No, I am not being facetious. Plato has a lot to say about the ideal conditions for nurturing elites, or what he called 'guardians'. So, of course, famously, did Edmund Burke.

> To be bred in a place of estimation; to see nothing low and sordid from one's infancy; to be taught to respect oneself; to be habituated to censorial inspection of the public eye . . . to stand upon such elevated ground as to be enabled to take a large view of the widespread and infinitely diversified combinations of men and affairs in a large society; to have leisure to read, to reflect, to converse; to be enabled to draw on the attention of the wise and learned, wherever they are to be found . . . these are the circumstances of men that form what I

---

* After living twelve years betwixt Beaconsfield and Gerrards Cross I am tempted to quote Matthew Arnold's infamously snobbish observations on the Victorian philistines of his day: 'Consider these people . . . their way of life, their habits, their manners, the very tones of their voice; look at them attentively; observe the literature they read, the things which give them pleasure, the words which come forth out their mouths, the thoughts which make the furniture of their minds; would any amount of wealth be worth having with the condition that one was to become just like these people by having it.'

call a natural aristocracy, without which there is no nation.

Nor does one need to go back to the eighteenth century or to classical Athens for such comments. For the great twentieth-century thinker and economist Joseph Schumpeter, in his famous *Capitalism, Socialism and Democracy* (1943), has this to say:

> There are many ways in which politicians of a sufficiently good quality can be secured. Thus far, however, experience seems to suggest that the only effective guarantee is in the existence of a social stratum itself a product of a severely selective process, that takes to politics as a matter of course. If such a stratum be neither too exclusive nor too accessible for the outsider and if it be strong enough to assimilate most of the elements it currently absorbs, it not only will present for the political career products of stocks that have successfully passed many tests in other fields – served, as it were, an apprenticeship in private affairs – but it will also increase their fitness by endowing them with traditions that embody experience, with a professional code and with a common fund of views.

Schumpeter's words 'Thus Far' were written during the war, but as far as I know there has been no evidence since then to suggest that we have found any better ways. Quite the opposite, judging by the quality of today's leaders. But when did you last hear a contemporary politician – even a Tory one – admit as much? Nor is this in the least surprising, since to do so would be committing political suicide.

While in the old days socialists argued, very reasonably, that it was the duty of the State to improve the conditions of the lower classes, and Old Tories argued, also very reasonably, that it was their party's duty to maintain the privileges of the upper classes (and the liberals made a powerful case for not feather-bedding either the Duke or the dustman), today all the parties agree, or pretend to agree, that it is the job of the State to do away with class altogether, quite regardless of the fact that our political institutions (c.f. Mao's head) grew out of that class system and have depended on it ever since for their health and strength.

But having been brought up among the upper class myself, perhaps it is only natural for me to be aware of that class's strengths and virtues rather than its limitations. I don't think so. For as it happens, fate dealt me a very mixed hand of class cards, which I like to think has made it easier for me than for others to achieve a degree of objectivity. But in case that is wishful thinking on my part, it is probably wisest to take the opportunity at the outset to lay my class cards face up on the table, so that readers of the essay can swallow it with as large or as little a pinch of salt as they deem desirable or necessary.

My grandfather, Alexander Koch de Gooreynd, came from Belgian banking stock, his father having emigrated here at the end of the nineteenth century. Having arrived, he bought a house in Belgrave Square and then built his wife another and tried – only being just nipped in the bud by the Astor family – to buy *The Times* from Lord North-cliffe. After sending my father to Eton and into the Irish Guards, my grandfather then put the final touches to my father's rites of passage into the upper class by arranging for him to marry my mother, granddaughter of the 12th Earl of Abingdon – a Catholic family connected by marriage to the Duke of Norfolk, secular head of the Catholic estab-lishment. The marriage, however, did not work since the couple were incompatible, my father wanting to lead the life of the idle rich and my mother, much the stronger character, determined to shoehorn him into English public life. The poor man was found a parliamentary constituency by our uncle Edmund Fitzalan, (younger brother of the Duke of Norfolk), the Tory Chief Whip at the time, and did his best – changing his name to Worsthorne* for the purpose – but it didn't work. And after several unsuccessful attempts, he gave up the struggle and the name. My mother, who despised the idle rich, never forgave him and they soon separated.

From then on, so terrified was my mother that my brother and I might follow in our father's self-indulgent footsteps that during our childhood we were scarcely ever allowed to see him. I remember being taken out from school in his yellow Rolls Royce,† equipped ahead of the times with a cocktail bar, at the most twice, and that, alas, was the total extent, until we came of age, of our contact. Not

---

* A village on his wife's family's estate in Lancashire.
† The original yellow Rolls Royce in the film of that name.

so much a role model, therefore, as an anti-role model. We were brought up to be as unlike our father as possible, even to the point of *not* being sent to Eton and *not* being allowed to join the Irish Guards.

Then, in the 1930s, our mother got her heart's desire. She married the man of her dreams, Montagu Norman, then the great interwar Governor of the Bank of England, as dedicated to public service as our father was to private pleasure. Norman, unlike our father, was Protestant, which meant divorce and remarriage in a registry office, both repugnant to our recusant Catholic relations, from whose presence my mother – to her great relief – and her children were summarily banished for life: for my brother and I, this meant, in turn, no more Christmases and holidays with Uncle Edmund at Cumberland Lodge, his grace-and-favour home in Windsor Park – where guests included George V and Queen Mary, as well as the then prime minister, Stanley Baldwin – or at Arundel Castle; and no more eavesdropping as our elders and betters discussed ad nauseam the Conversion of England, the future of the Catholic schools, and other such burning public issues of the day. But instead, being thenceforward under Montagu Norman's roof, we soon became equally accustomed to hear talk about more secular public issues – the Gold Standard, unemployment, etc., with visitors like Dr Schacht, Hitler's economic guru, Sir John Reith, the first Director General of the BBC, and Maynard Keynes. So from a very early age, *res publica*, 'the public thing', was part of our lives.

I can remember quite clearly when I was made aware

17

that it was not part of everybody else's life. The parents of a fellow pupil at my prep school had taken me out and in the course of the outing my friend's father, who was in the rag trade, had waxed indignant about a Neville Chamberlain Budget. Always anxious to find some precociously grown-up subject to write about to my mother in my weekly letter home, I passed on this conversation, mentioning in particular the father's objection to a tax rise that would hit the retail trade particularly hard, only to receive a long hand-written letter – the first and the last – from the Governor himself. Sadly, I haven't kept the text, but its gist left a lasting mark. The Chancellor's job, he emphasized, was not to please the rag trade, or any other private interest, but rather to take care of the nation's solvency. A good Budget was almost by definition an unpopular Budget. He went on to cite his friend Walter Lippmann's view that it was a government's job to tax, conscript, command and prohibit, punish, and balance the budget, none of which responsibilities could usually be safely fulfilled without offending many individual members of the public. Inevitably, the conflict between the public interest and the private interest was most acute in time of war, when the balance had to be got right between the public interest in victory and the private interest of millions of mothers and fathers that their boys should return home alive; but in peacetime, too, there could be almost equally agonizing conflicts and he instanced his own recent duty at the Bank of England to take actions in the national interest that had inflicted cruel suffering on the unemployed.

Very recently, in Louis Menand's excellent book *The Metaphysical Club* – mostly about late nineteenth- and early twentieth-century American philosophers – I came across a ruling of the famous American Civil War veteran and Supreme Court Justice Oliver Wendell Holmes, who was also one of my stepfather's correspondents, and its chilling note had such a familiar ring that I am sure it was also included in that letter. Certainly it is in its spirit and comes in the course of a 1927 opinion by Holmes about a Virginian law permitting the involuntary sterilization of mentally incompetent persons. Menand rightly describes it as Holmes's most 'notorious opinion'* and it went as follows:

> We have seen more than once that the public welfare may well call upon the best citizens for their lives.† It would be strange if it could not call upon those who already sap the strength of the State for these lesser sacrifices.

Whether or not that was the same quotation as the one recommended to me by my stepfather I shall never know; but, if not, it was certainly another equally stupefying.

And then at about the same time, as if to pile Pelion on Ossa, the critic John Davenport – whose war work was to

---

* The adjective 'obnoxious' might have been even more apt.
† He was referring to the terrible losses incurred by both sides in the American Civil War.

teach English at Stowe for the duration – recommended me to read Robert Burton's *The Anatomy of Melancholy*, wherein I came across a passage that included the following quotation from Boethius:

> If any were visited with the falling sickness, madness, gout, leprosy, or any such dangerous disease, which was likely to be propagated from the father to the son, he was instantly gelded; a woman kept from all company of men; and if by chance, having some such disease, she were found to be with child, she with her brood were buried alive: and this was done for the common good, *lest the whole nation should be injured or corrupted* [my italics].

To which Burton had added:

> A severe doom, you will say, and not to be used amongst Christians, yet more to be looked into than it is. For now, by our too much facility in this kind, in giving way for all to marry that will, too much liberty and indulgence in tolerating all sorts, there is a vast confusion of hereditary diseases, no family secure, no man almost, free from some grievous infirmity or other, when no choice is had.

It was a heady brew. Clearly somebody, 'lest the whole nation should be injured or corrupted', had to do the nation's dirty work; had to authorize difficult and sometimes cruel actions for the common good; had to be on the side of realism against sentimentality; had to resist giving way not only to every grievance (which was relatively easy) but also to manifestly worthy causes as well; had to rub society's nose in the painful realities of keeping a great nation on course. No less clearly, careerist politicians – whose careers depended on retaining popular favour – were the last people who could be relied upon to grasp these nettles. So who were these indispensable somebodies who had to bear these public burdens? The inference from my stepfather's letter was unavoidable: those indispensable somebodies most definitely included me.

I don't remember being in the least pleased by this realization, still less proud. It seemed, at first, a terrifying prospect. All my schoolboy inclinations at Stowe were inclined towards private pleasures – particularly the pleasure of burying my head in a book – and against team spirit, which was the boarding-school idea of public duty. The last thing I wanted – at any rate in these early years – was to be made a prefect. Neither did I want to forgo the protection that the prefects – or at least the decent ones – provided the weak and cowardly (i.e. me) against the bullies.* So I wanted

---

* Robert Kee, the author and broadcaster, has recently told me he was a senior prefect in my House at Stowe in the mid 1930s and remembers having to come to my rescue. Someone had rushed up to him to say that a new boy called Worsthorne minor had been strapped into a laundry basket that was about to be tumbled down a steep staircase. Just in time Kee was able to intervene to save my neck!

the best of both worlds: authority figures who at one and the same time both protected me and left me alone; who came to my aid in emergencies but otherwise allowed me to mind my own business. Officious busybody prefects who kept an eye on one all the time were more a liability than an asset. But unofficious prefects who noticed what was going on from a corner of the eye were the opposite. Even more to be desired were the few older boys who turned down the office of prefect but were natural authority figures on the side of justice and order requiring, by virtue of strong individual character, no official badge of office. Those paragons, however, are always very few on the ground and, not being among them, I did eventually accept being made a prefect, because one of that office's privileges was frequent contact with the great founding headmaster, J. F. Roxburgh, who exercised authority with the lightest of reins in the manner of a connoisseur who appreciates quality and style in all its forms, as much in the dilettante aesthete who refuses to play games as in the captain of the school rugger XV who refuses to do anything else. He believed a well-ordered boarding school should not aim to turn out leadership material of a uniform sort but quality material for every different walk of life – quality top dogs and quality bottom dogs, quality politicians and quality voters, and even quality revolutionaries. 'Don't talk of a ruling class,' he would say. 'Call it a quality class, a class that contributes to the good society just as much by "being" as by "doing".'

As for how Stowe was different from, say, Eton, I think JF would have replied along the following lines: that whereas Eton had seen its function as that of civilizing primarily the sons of the old ruling class, and only secondarily the sons of the nouveaux riches whose parents wanted their offspring 'aristocratized', Stowe saw its function as that of turning out *humane* and gentrified meritocrats who would not take it for granted, or give the impression that they took it for granted, that they were 'born to rule'. What JF wanted, in short, was the Etonian spirit in a more egalitarian frame, or, as he put it, 'Etonians in grey flannels rather than in the archaic white tie and tails'. One was never left in doubt at Stowe that competitive individualism and equality of opportunity were the waves of the future; but neither was one left in doubt that it was the duty of an Old Stoic to ride these waves not just to his own personal advantage, but also to the advantage of the nation as a whole. *Oblige*, yes: JF tried hard to instil that; but he was rather less emphatic about *noblesse*. A gentrified or patrician meritocracy, not unlike the Wasp ascendancy on the East Coast of America, was JF's ideal, which to some extent he achieved in such Old Stoics of my generation as Noel Annan,[*] Robert Kee, Tony Quinton, and, quintessentially, the figure of Nicko Henderson, the most relaxed, informal, and least stuffy top English Ambassador ever.

Put like that, my stepfather's idea of public duties seemed to me rather less frighteningly high-powered and much more acceptably low-key, especially after – at the instigation of Stowe's charismatic history tutor, Bill McElwee – reading

---

[*] Annan wrote the authorized biography of JF.

Alexis de Tocqueville's great classic *Democracy in America*. For Tocqueville gave a commonsensical, un-Hobbesian rationale to the ideal of aristocracy: not so much as a body of superior beings bred to exercise power over the people but as a body of men whose dignified and leisured circumstances made them most likely to exercise power in the public interest, mainly because, in their case, the public interest and the private interest – by reason of the aristocracy's greater stake in the country – was so nearly indistinguishable. 'Among aristocratic nations', Tocqueville wrote,

> a man almost always knows his forefathers and respects them; he thinks he already sees his remote descendants and he loves them. He willingly imposes duties on himself towards the former and the latter, and he will *frequently sacrifice his own personal gratifications to those who went before and to those who will come after him* [my italics].

Tocqueville's was a down-to-earth utilitarian justification for aristocracy – 'that it worked'. In France, where aristocracy had been degraded by the French monarchy, aristocracy led to revolution; in England, where the aristocracy had degraded the monarchy, aristocracy led to order and justice. The English aristocracy, he wrote, 'is perhaps the most liberal that ever existed and no body of men has ever uninterruptedly furnished so many honourable and enlightened individuals for the government of a country'.

In the light of what we now think we know about the lamentable state of the English ruling class in the 1920s and 1930s, Tocqueville's idealistic assumption about its merits may indeed seem quite ludicrously out of date. Certainly today's conventional wisdom has it that the golden chivalry of England was all mown down while leading their men into battle in the Great War, leaving only the dross behind. Nobody who has read the socialite Chips Channon's interwar diaries, which give a picture of hedonistic irresponsibility and self-indulgence in high places of almost Nero-like proportions, would be inclined to doubt this; and Evelyn Waugh's famous interwar novel *Vile Bodies* confirms that impression. So does Edward VIII's pathetic abdication, usually portrayed as *the* prime example of that age's spirit of irresponsible hedonism. In my recollection, however, that decadent impression is profoundly misleading. For surely, with the benefit of hindsight, we can now recognize that the truly remarkable aspect of the abdication was not the King's irresponsible hedonism but the Establishment's revulsion – strong enough to force him off the throne – against his irresponsible hedonism. Both my old Catholic family and my new Norman family circles played prominent parts in this reaction. It was my uncle Edmund Fitzalan, for example, who helped persuade Stanley Baldwin that the King would have to abdicate and my stepfather Montagu Norman who exercised the same kind of pressure – not that he actually needed much pressure – on Neville Chamberlain. If one wants an example of how a well-functioning Establishment can serve the public interest, the despatch of

Edward VIII provides it in spades. But that is only one small illustration of how, in my recollection, the achievements of the governing class in the 1920s and 1930s, at any rate on the home front, have not yet received their fair share of acclamation.

It was an intensely difficult period. In the aftermath of the horrors of the First World War, the raw passions of democracy, inflamed both by totalitarian temptations from the far Left as from the far Right, were threatening to burn the house down. If Britain's parliamentary democracy was to have a chance of surviving, it had to come up with an alternative that could also catch the public's imagination. That is what the great conservative leader and Prime Minister, Stanley Baldwin, succeeded in doing long before Roosevelt did something of the same order with his New Deal in the United States. In a whole series of speeches of incomparable eloquence, both inside and outside Parliament, Baldwin sought to link patriotic pride to the uniquely English set of gentlemanly rules and conduct towards others.* He appealed to the best of the working class and the best of the industrialists to prove to the world that in the self-sacrificial, altruistic ideal of the English gentleman, unique to this country, lay the only safe way forward. As a result of English history, he argued, a unique system of

---

* My memory of Baldwin's achievements has been revived by a majestically fair account given by the historian Philip Williamson in *Public and Private Doctrine*, a collection of essays presented to Maurice Cowling and edited by Michael Bentley (Cambridge University Press, 1993).

mutual obligations and duties had been evolved that could and must be called upon to help the country escape the looming horrors of class war. Let the best among the working-class leaders and among the industrialists defy Marx by showing that in England both were capable, like true aristocrats, of behaving nobly, not so as to facilitate the dominion of one particular class but in the interest of serving the country as a whole. Baldwin's constant evocation of England's rural arcadia was not due to any sentimentally nostalgic desire to put the industrial clock back. How could it be, given his own ironmaster's background? No, it was due to his belief that in the pre-industrial centuries some unique quality of trust had been engendered that could once again be enlisted to see the nation through difficult and dangerous times. Class war, socialism, fascism were un-English ideas, only suitable, if suitable at all, for foreign countries unlucky enough not to have developed the English gentlemanly habits of conciliation and compromise that would see us through the problems of the twentieth century, just as they had seen us through the problems of previous centuries. Greedy acquisitiveness was the enemy wherever it reared its ugly head, particularly, of course, among the rich. Baldwin abhorred 'the hard faced millionaires who had done well out of the war'. In fact it was he who coined the phrase, not Keynes, and he hated ostentatious displays of wealth. The word 'service' was central to his discourse, especially the service owed by the rich, the privileged, and the well educated, who were repeatedly adjured to put human rights before the rights of property. Britain was, in one of his phrases, 'a noble democracy'. Even if industrialists and trade union leaders everywhere else knew only how to behave like 'robber barons', in Britain at least they could be relied upon to behave like Christian gentlemen. That was the *ideal* he preached and, in his courteous treatment of Labour Party leaders and trade union leaders, also practised, according them a public respect he went out of his way not to accord to many of the industrialists.

Montagu Norman agreed with every word. He, too, believed that the wealthy classes should place love of country before money; that wealth involved stewardship; that industrial employers should aim to act as trustees for the whole community; and, above all, that employees were only as good as their employers. He, too, deplored managers and directors who were interested primarily in their salaries and fees – people we now call fat cats – and refused to have them at his table, believing that flaunting vulgar ostentation offered revolutionaries their best justification.*

Like most public-school boys of the period, at any rate those at the public schools, I was deeply affected by Baldwin's great speeches, one of which I was taken to hear in a packed and enthusiastic Albert Hall. Collections of his speeches were presented as school prizes and bishops used quotations from them as a text for their sermons. His main theme was very simple: that instead of looking abroad for grand new ideologies to solve the problems of the twentieth

---

* Alongside Beaverbrook and Rothermere in his rogues' gallery were to be found the German industrialists Krupp and Thyssen.

century, all classes should instead buckle down, in the time-honoured way, to do their duty, which, of course, is what, when the war came, most of them did. So whatever can be said by way of criticism of Baldwin for not attending to the country's material rearmament, nobody can justly deny him the credit for carrying out an exercise in moral rearmament quite unparalleled in the nation's history.

W. H. Auden's jibe about the 1930s being a 'low dis-honest decade', therefore, does not at all accord with my own recollection. I remember it as a decade when the con-cept of duty* was stretched to cover pretty well everything; when selfishness was regarded as the mark of the beast, the root of all moral failure; when altruism was held to be the root of all virtue; and when, under Baldwin's spell, those aspiring to govern were adjured to dedicate themselves, if not to the service of God, then with all the more fervour to the service of their fellow men. Rereading these speeches today – dismissed at the time by intellectuals of the Right and the Left as impractical and unrealistic – I have to say that they seem to have stood the test of time far better than the writings of those same intellectuals, which now read like the ravings of madmen. In any case, if the 1930s really were such a 'low and dishonest decade', one question has to be asked. How did it come to pass that of all the countries

---

* I have always suspected that the motive of the upper-class traitors who spied for the Soviet Union was not so much disgust at the upper-class privileges of the time as a rebellion against the number of duties – which boys at public schools in those days were never allowed to forget – accompanying those privileges.

that lived through those years, Britain, alone among the great European powers, escaped relatively unscathed from the corrosions of fascism and communism and went into the war against Hitler so relatively united and with such relatively high national morale? While Churchill's courageous oratory was certainly part of the answer, the Baldwin balm was also a blessing beyond price.

The support of the ruling classes for the Chamberlain policy of appeasement is much more difficult to cast in a good light. But here again, from my particular viewpoint, it did not strike me then, and it does not strike me now, as in the least 'low' or 'dishonest' in the ordinary sense of those words. My stepfather, who had a won a DSO in the Boer War, stood foursquare behind Chamberlain's appeasement policy, not out of weak unwillingness to face up to the reality of war – his long talks in Berlin and London with Dr Schacht, Hitler's economic adviser, had dissolved all illusions on that score – but rather out of an equally strong determination to be realistic about the consequences for Britain of going to war with Hitler. His charge against Churchill was that while he was telling the British people the truth about the gravity of the former reality, he was grossly deceiving them about the gravity of the second, which could not fail, he believed, to be the end of Britain as a great and independent power, win or lose the war. Going to war could well be Churchill's 'finest hour', Norman used to say, but for Britain it would be the beginning of the end. Like Robert Fossett, the fictional hero of Christopher Hollis's book, *The Death of a Gentleman* –

which came out in 1943 – Norman always 'shuddered at the folly of those who talked as if a war would be merely a matter of beating Hitler, and that then, that evil removed, the world would go on its comfortable way of progress, like a man who has had an aggravating tooth removed at the dentist. Starting a war was much more like starting a glacier. The world was full of disruptive, nihilistic forces, and, once the ice began to move, none could say how far it would travel, nor what at the last would survive its catastrophe.' In Norman's view, therefore, the appeasers were not a lot of unpatriotic poltroons, as against the Churchillians who were patriotic statesman willing to grasp nettles. Rather the opposite. It was the appeasers who were grasping the most frightening nettle of all, which was that the only way for Britain to survive as a great power, and the only way for the old conservative Europe to survive, was to avoid a war with Hitler, even if this did involve paying the horribly high price of abandoning Eastern Europe and the Jews to a terrible fate. Of course in the light of Churchill's victory in 1945, appeasement did come to seem shamefully defeatist. But surely, in the light of what we know of the decline and disintegration of Britain in the last half of the twentieth century, and its likely disappearance to all great effects and noble purposes, except as foot soldiers in an American army, in the first half of the twenty-first century; and in the light, moreover, of what, in spite of Churchill's war, *did* happen to the Jews and to the East Europeans, one can now see that the appeasers were not acting out of cowardice but out of a kind of sober courage, by comparison with which

Churchill's eagerness to embrace war begins to seem almost irresponsibly vainglorious.*

Another difficulty for the reputation of the appeasers is that, because they were in power in the 1930s, they are still associated in the public mind with the decadence of high society in that decade. In fact, however, the leading appeasers – Baldwin, Chamberlain, Norman, and others – much less deserved to be tarred with that brush than many of the anti-appeasers, like the financially greedy Churchill, the unashamedly lecherous Duff Cooper, and the almost brazenly dishonest Robert Boothby. The difficulty here is that the true muscle of the 1930s ruling class did not frequent high society, did not go to grand balls or Belgrave Square parties. Hence the erroneous impression that the space at the top of the tree in the 1930s was entirely filled by social butterflies. If Norman had kept a diary, however, it would have given a very different and more impressive picture, as my brother and I have good cause to remember. For his public service standards, and those of his whole world, were Spartan to a fault, or to what my brother and I judged to be a fault. No luxuries were tolerated, and strict economies enforced. So when I became keen on riding at

---

* Sebastian Haffner, in his biography of Churchill, even goes so far as to suggest that Churchill, in order to destroy Hitler, would have been recklessly willing 'to sacrifice Britain's existence', just as fourteen years earlier he would have been recklessly willing 'to crush the General Strike by unleashing civil war' – neither dispositions being 'patriotic' in any reasonable understanding of the word. *Churchill: Life and Times* (Haus, 2003; originally published in German, 1967).

my preparatory school, and wrote asking for riding boots, my mother sent me a pair of her own – far too pointed at the toe for my comfort – with the raised heels sawn off. And such was the importance placed on not disturbing the Governor's concentration on his public duties that we were kept out of his way during school holidays in a country cottage of our own, with our own butler and cook – more fun in theory than in practice, since our mother, who shared her second husband's priorities, was seldom present. In fact, domestic felicity and family life seldom got a look in.

Born into an upper-middle-class banking family of long standing and educated at Eton – which, unlike my father, he hated – and at King's College Cambridge, Norman dedicated all his waking hours to the City of London, living austerely, almost ascetically, and eschewing wine, women (until he met my mother) and song so as to be able to give his all to his work. He was, at all times, a pillar of rectitude, imposing on the City the highest standards of integrity. The idle-rich, Chips Channon kind of society appalled him and he deplored the loving attention given by the media to this debauched minority, rightly regarding their antics as obscenely objectionable at a time of mass unemployment brought about very largely, of course, by his own tight fiscal policies, harshly imposed, he always believed, in the long term 'public interest'.

His own life, as I say, was exemplary in this regard. Whereas most bankers went to the City in chauffeur-driven Rolls Royces, he travelled by tube from Notting Hill Gate to the Bank, causing quite a sensation by so doing. Indeed the spectacle of this tall figure with a Charles I beard, season ticket tucked into the ribbon of his silk hat worn at a jaunty angle, descending into the underground at 8.30 a.m. sharp and ascending thirty minutes later at the Bank – where the buses were held up to allow the Governor to cross Threadneedle Street – became almost as much of a tourist attraction as the Changing of the Guard outside Buckingham Palace. His hobby was to design and build furniture in the Art Deco style, and although he inherited two country houses, he occupied only a garden cottage in one, where he made a point of coming down to dinner in slippers and bare feet and eating simple fare. When the Second World War came, almost nothing had to change. Even in peacetime, we were already living, *by choice*, on a war footing.

As for hobbies, his favourite one was snubbing newspaper proprietors because they exaggerated – in search of circulation-building copy – the importance of the decadent elements in high society, thereby irresponsibly dissolving the bonds of mutual sympathy and respect that should naturally exist between rich and poor, governors and governed. He was fond of saying that they had a vested interest in barbarism because civilization did not sell newspapers. Lord Beaverbrook, for example, was never allowed to cross the threshold. Norman's secretary was instructed to refuse all his importuning. Naturally that was not the picture – as insecure interlopers desperate for recognition – the newspapers chose to give of where their proprietors stood in the social pecking order, but this was how they were looked down on from our particular pinnacle. When Lord and Lady

Kemsley, then the owners of the *Sunday Times*, wrote to say that they were looking forward to being fellow passengers on a transatlantic liner my mother and Norman were planning to take to New York, my mother immediately arranged to cancel their own booking. Nobody today would dare to give the Murdochs or even the discredited Blacks the same kind of brush-off. Whereas today the media chiefs are the lords of all they survey, with none – not even the Prime Minister – daring to say them nay, then, thanks to the class system, there were still a few who would tell the cheeky urchins 'to keep off the grass'.

Nor was Norman in any way unique. All his closest friends, Sir Warren Fisher and Sir Richard Hopkins, both in their time Head of the Treasury, and Sir John Reith, Director General of the BBC, were equally driven by the same classical republican ideals, which insisted that the highest purpose of man was to sacrifice himself, and his family, on the altar of the common weal – clearly far too lofty an ideal for the common man and only to be expected of the very uncommon man: the active citizen brought up to meet these exacting standards, either from birth or at least after five Spartan years at an English public school. Aristocracy, in this tradition, was much more a burden to be taken up than a privilege to be enjoyed, much more a sacrifice than an indulgence, Being born with a silver spoon in your mouth meant keeping your nose to the grindstone for life.

My mother completely shared Norman's values. Not only was she a member of the London County Council, calling her racing greyhound Hammersmith (Hammy for short) after her constituency, but also a JP and social worker and, when the war began, a founder, under Lady Reading, of the Women's Voluntary Service (WVS), which is still going strong as the WRVS. I remember as a teenager, in the absence of any suitable female, having to model various possible uniforms for my mother to choose from – and hats too. After the war, she also became president of the Mental Health Association, forcing James the butler, a Great War veteran, much to his embarrassment, to shake the Association's collection box in all the local pubs for what, at the time, was a most unpopular cause. Like Norman himself, she looked down from a great height on high society, quoting the great Lord Salisbury's description of its members – which she thought her mother, Lady Alice, might have actually heard – as 'dwarfed, languid, nerveless, emasculated dilettantes'. No efforts were spared to deter her sons from sinking so low.

Lady Alice was another formative influence, and in the same league. Widowed in her early age by the death of her second husband, Major Robert Reyntiens, a dashing Belgian soldier who had been ADC (some said pimp) to King Leopold of the Belgians, she inherited shortly thereafter what remains of the great recusant Towneley property, stretching from Burnley in Lancashire to the Yorkshire border town of Todmorden at the other end of the wild Cliviger Gorge, which figures so romantically in Harrison Ainsworth's novel *The Lancashire Witches*. The house itself, Towneley Hall, a massive fortress dating back to the fifteenth century, had been bought by the Burnley Corporation and turned into a museum, which meant that the only available house on the estate for my grandmother to live in was the agent's hideous late-Victorian villa, Dyneley, overlooking the gorge. Although the country was still rugged, much of its beauty had been tarnished by coal mining and the smoke-belching chimneys of the cotton mills – one of the reasons why so many of the old Lancashire families had moved south to less grimy climes. Strongly disapproving of absentee land-lords, my grandmother decided to reverse the shameless exodus. It was a brave decision. Towneley estate was an oasis of old agricultural Lancashire in a great desert of indus-trial blight. Cliviger village, above which Dyneley perched, served the local mill and at the break of a summer's day the sound of clogs could be heard in the distance. My grand-mother's smart friends could not understand why she wanted to go and live in such an outlandish place where there was no hunting and no social life – by which they meant no neighbours of the right sort. But she did not *want* to. It was a matter of duty. For six hundred years, since the time of Edward III, the Towneleys kept the flame of Catholicism burning bright in Lancashire, cruelly persecuted at times for their fidelity to the Old Faith, and my grandmother could think of no good reason not to continue honouring this ancient obligation. Moving north was certainly a great wrench. She loved the pleasures of fashionable life – her sister, Lady Goonie, a leading member of 'the Souls', was married to Winston Churchill's brother, Jack; but no sooner did she inherit than she packed up in London and moved to Dyneley, where she gave over her life to good works – running the local Girl Guides, sitting on the County Council and on the Bench, and reviving the Towneley chapel in Burnley.

Admittedly Montagu Norman and my mother's family were exceptionally, almost obsessively, public spirited and high principled and therefore potentially a threat to liberty because of their excess of zeal. But the great advantage of the old hereditary upper class was that, being a family association, it included all sorts – including its fair share of dandies and dilettantes – and Montagu Norman's younger brother, R. C. Norman, who was allowed to live in the big house, was as elegantly and civilizedly relaxed as Montagu was driven and single minded. Ronnie Norman was what Max Weber called a *grand rentier*, entirely detached from the source of his income, entirely uninvolved in the day-to-day running of any organization – an agent ran his estate – and therefore able to look at the world from a great distance. By 'detached' Weber did not mean impersonal; he meant 'un-embattled' and 'un-embroiled'. Most of us, until we are retired, think about everything with only half our minds, the other half being engaged in worrying about some unfinished business in the office or, if we are a farmer, about the weather or the price of grain. Ronnie Norman was not embattled or embroiled in this way at all. He occupied a more serene sphere. Not that he was idle: he was a great patron of the arts, a great reader, Chairman of the BBC*

---

* Such was his quiet authority and charm that he was able to persuade an alcoholic Director-General to retire from the corporation without any scandalous publicity.

(then, as now, a part-time job), a devoted father of five, with a wide circle of close friends, including his old Cambridge contemporary, the historian G. M. Trevelyan, who later became Master of Trinity College, and his neighbour, the sculptor Henry Moore; but in all these roles it was his serenity, his detachment, that made him so exceptionally valuable, as it did in his role as brother of Montagu Norman. It was a good sibling combination since at weekends the younger brother's passion for domestic felicity perfectly complemented the older's passion for public duty, and vice versa, thereby helping to ensure that in one upper-class family the interest of the State and the interest of the individual were both kept in happy balance. One such miniscule concentration of unofficial power and influence, of course, would count for little; but multiplied into tens of thousands of comparable grandee family concentrations spread across the land, all coming from the same background, with many actually related, certainly did add up to something.

What was that something? I think it was an alternative vision of a good life; a vision beyond the range of the bourgeois or proletarian imagination. In this world, there was no sense of having been frightened into public life by fear of socialism, or driven into it on behalf of the workers. So far as it is humanly possible, 'interest' did not come into it. Because the Normans, who had had it 'made' from birth, did not have to better their own lot, they felt in duty bound, in their different fashions, to fight for the public good. In no sense did they think this made them superior to those who came from less fortunate circumstances. Comparable public spirit, I was brought up to believe, could be found in all classes; the only difference was that it was easier for some to be active democrats – that is, to participate directly in the nation's government and law making and to lead a socially responsible life – than it was for others. This was the idea of aristocracy transformed into democratic terms. Far from the existence of a privileged group spared from the strivings and struggles of their fellow citizens being incompatible with democracy, it was *in practice*, we believed, a necessary condition of democracy. Has this ceased to be true? I rather doubt it. For while Britain is more democratic socially today than it was, I doubt whether it is more democratic politically, in the sense of more people feeling effectively in charge of the State. Then, a class with connections stretching across the whole kingdom felt in charge; today, that feeling would seem to be limited to a succession of small groups of political professionals and political journalists, here today and gone tomorrow, with few connections outside Westminster.

Another lesson from those days also sticks in my mind: the extent to which an hereditary aristocracy, being a civil association made up of families, helped to keep the lines of communication open between the various self-contained and often feuding elites – political, bureaucratic, artistic, religious, sporting, and so on. Again, the extended Norman family (or firm) was a good example of this, since house parties would often include senior members of most of the various elites – one in the Cabinet Office, one in the War Office, one in the City, one in the legal profession, one a racing enthusiast – whose weekday narrowness of vision and exclusive concern with their own separate sections of the governing order would quickly dissolve, allowing the unifying ties of kinship to re-exert their hold. Nowadays, of course, British society is incomparably more compartmentalized than it used to be, and members of the various elites only intermingle at such artificial gatherings as 'interdisciplinary conferences', international congresses organized by the great foundations, or in special committees set up for that purpose. But, as T. S. Eliot put it, 'Men who meet only for definite serious purposes, and on official occasions, do not wholly meet.' That ease of communication that comes naturally in the drawing room or in the salon or in the club cannot be artificially recreated in the symposium or seminar. Even the language is different. Whereas in the former it tended to be urbane, witty, and free-ranging, in the latter it tends to be boring, technical, and focused. Nietzsche made the point well when he said that the problem with the German language is that it developed not in courts and salons, as did English and French, but in universities and seminaries.

The measure of aristocracy, which in those days was mixed into a democratic soil, also did wonders for keeping down bureaucracy, which is one of the most worryingly invasive weeds in the democratic garden – only slightly less worrying than that other potentially poisonous growth, a standing army. For aristocracy and bureaucracy are natural enemies, as Matthew Arnold explained:

Aristocratic bodies have no taste for a very imposing executive, or for a very active and penetrating domestic administration. They have a sense of equality among themselves, and of constituting in themselves what is greatest and most dignified in the realm, which makes their pride revolt against the overshadowing greatness and dignity of a commanding executive. They have a temper of independence, and a habit of uncontrolled action, which makes them impatient of encountering, in the management of the interior concerns of the country, the machinery and regulations of a superior and peremptory power.

In other words, it is in the nature of aristocrats to want 'to take jumped-up jacks in office down a peg or two'. In my childhood in the 1930s the grown-ups were always waging a relentless war against 'faceless bureaucrats', both religious and secular, either on their own behalf or on behalf of their many dependants. After hunting and shooting, it was their favourite sport. The less privileged classes, therefore, needed to feel no inhibition about turning to aristocrats for help. They were knocking on open palace doors. And in those days grandees were easy to locate and very far from being anonymous. Manifestly it was not an ideal system. But the present more democratic system of writing to newspapers, or of collecting masses of individual signatures for petitions, or of writing to the ombudsman, are not ideal either. For example, the residents of the village in which I now live are always writing to various 'inspectors' begging them to turn down some new threat or other – a new motorway service station, for example – seldom receiving more satisfaction than an official acknowledgement with an indecipherable signature. Of course, in theory, democratic numbers should be enough to impress central or local government officials; but in practice, I suspect, nothing will ever again be as effective, in this respect, as was the commanding voice of a member of the English upper class, ideally female.

Unhappy as some of my formative experiences were, all in all, it was a pretty good soil for someone wanting to go into public life to spring from; not altogether unlike those recommended by Burke and Schumpeter as ideal for nurturing future rulers. Right from the start I had felt at home – literally so – with the powerful who, therefore, held no terrors for me; right from the start I had had a sense of being part of a public process, of belonging to a civil association bound together by shared memories and traditions and – such being the degree of intermarriage – shared blood; above all, by an inherited and nurtured sense of public duty. Whereas for most citizens the idea of aspiring to national government seemed out of this world, beyond their dreams, for me it seemed the natural thing to do; rather more natural than not going into politics.

In the event, only one impediment stopped me: a lack of private means. Being a younger son, such money and property as there was went to my older brother, and it was he, rather than I, who could afford to take up public duties, culminating in his case – transcending even my grandmother's record – in his becoming Lord Lieutenant of

Lancashire. Being a younger son, I had instead to think of earning my own living, which soon lowered my sights. For to go into public life without independent means, or the spivvish knack of effortlessly making fast money – neither of which I possessed – necessitates in the aspirant a degree of unhealthily obsessive careerism, which thankfully I also lacked. My ambition, as befits anyone who is not financially independent, did not extend further than keeping myself and my young family afloat. Local government and local public service was just about possible, but – wholly on material grounds – national politics was a bridge too far. So I did the next best thing and joined *The Times*, which in those days was a kind of auxiliary public service, at least compared to the rest of Fleet Street. Those who worked for the paper saw the world from the general point of view of a member of the ruling class, whose judgements came from proximity to government rather than from the specialist outlook of the professional journalist. And while *Times* journalists did not rule out fierce disagreement with what a particular government might be doing, they did rule out any disagreement that might threaten the national interest. In writing a leader, one was always constrained to weigh one's words with due consideration to the fact that the chancelleries of Europe* would be reading them. To that degree, *Times* leaders were State papers, far more than

---

* Not only the chancelleries of Europe since my first evening's work on the imperial and foreign sub-editor's table was entirely given over to checking the correct Arabic spelling of the names of the entire Sudanese government.

mere journalism, as I learnt to my cost since it meant that all one's best phrases and arguments were ruthlessly removed. Something of this same sense of public responsibility could be found at the top end of all the professions in those days. I remember asking my stepfather what was the most important part of being Governor of the Bank of England. His reply was: 'preventing dogs from fouling those legendary streets which fools suppose are paved with gold'. It was not enough just to be a good banker, or a good journalist – or a good lawyer, sportsman, or landowner, for that matter – since over and above all these specialist responsibilities there were the added obligations arising from membership of a privileged governing class. With the demise of that class, that extra sense of obligation has diminished, and nowhere more than at *The Times*. Nowadays *Times* journalists, like journalists in general, are closer to government than ever before. But where once upon a time this proximity was used to encourage greater understanding, on the principle of *tout comprendre, c'est tout pardonner*, today it is used the better to take good aim at the ship of state before blowing her out of the water.

In any case, to work on *The Times* had been a vague ambition of mine ever since my Aunt Nell, with whom I used to stay while down from Cambridge early in the war, used me as a messenger to take up to London on Sunday night the letters, written over the weekend, with which she regularly bombarded her friends and relations in high places, one of whom happened then to be the editor of *The Times*, Geoffrey Dawson, who, finding a likely lad with the right connections in the anteroom to his office, had, in the way things used to happen in those days, taken me out to supper at Pratts. The rest, as they say, is history.

Not that I ever became a journalist in the contemporary adversarial sense, which allows for no scruples about rocking the boat. Having been brought up as a member of the governing class, for me it was a question of getting the balance right: the balance between causing mischief, which was permitted, and creating mayhem, which was not. No doubt I often failed to keep that balance but, unlike most of the journalists today, it was not through want of trying; of trying, that is, to put the public interest in discretion, and not washing too much dirty linen in public, before careerist self-indulgence and self-interest in 'telling all'.

But even that may overstate my motive. For morality and manners are so intertwined in England that it is often difficult to know, in any particular case, which carries the most clout. In my journalistic career, it could well have been manners, since I would often invite VIPs to lunch at the Connaught Grill with every intention of trying to beguile them with sweetmeats into betraying State secrets and then, at the last moment over the coffee, brandy, and cigars draw back from asking the scoop-producing awkward question for fear of spoiling what until then had been such a convivial occasion. Most likely, therefore, I never spilled any valuable beans because I never had any to spill.

So in spite of not being myself in a financial position to transcend the demands of career advancement or organizational competitiveness, I nevertheless felt inescapably bound – almost against my will – to behave like a gentleman. Pride in gentlemanly status took precedence over greed and even over ambition. Gentlemanliness in those days was a high calling that a few tried to live up to because of genuine virtue, never cutting corners or taking the easy options and always obeying not so much the letter as the spirit of the law and spurning opportunities to make quick and easy money in favour of the more honourably won and longer-term gains; others because, being so well off, it was no skin off their nose to be high principled; but most, like me, did so out of a desire not to lose caste or, like an ever greater number, out of a desire to gain caste.

Most certainly it was not the most democratic way to fashion a governing class. For by linking the widespread desire to acquire social status to the performance of public duties and the upholding of professional values, it almost guaranteed and legitimized the continuation of hierarchy and social inequality. So if equality of access is to be regarded as essential for any morally acceptable system of recruitment into the political elite, this old way definitely does not pass that test. But judged by whether it serves the public interest by producing a regular supply of top-rank politicians, public servants, and professionals, did it pass that test? Tocqueville's answer, as we have already seen, was emphatically affirmative: but that was in the early nineteenth century, and even then he was worried that England's class system might not be able to do justice to the victims of the Industrial Revolution. Hence he qualified his encomium for the English aristocracy by writing 'the miseries and privations of her poor almost equal [her aristocracy's] power and renown', which was certainly true at the time Tocqueville wrote; since then, however, there have been almost two centuries of progress for the poor under a social system that even to this day, is still accused of being unegalitarian and class ridden. So if the welfare of the poor was the only complaint Tocqueville had against the English class system – and it was – that fault has by now been rectified, at least as much as it has been rectified in the supposedly more classless societies of the United States and continental Europe. Yet there are still many voices here, now coming as much from the New Conservatives as from the New Labourites, in favour of even more anti-elitism and even more social equality, regardless of the fact that in the last two centuries as much has been done to eliminate what Tocqueville saw as the main virtue of England's class system – its unrivalled success at furnishing honourable and enlightened men for public service – as has been done to eliminate what he saw as its main vice – a lack of concern about poverty.

Does this make sense? Will the war against poverty, which has been waged with astonishing success under what has remained of the old class system, be prosecuted more effectively by eliminating even more completely that old system? I don't believe so. I believe that getting rid of the last vestiges of the old social system – the system which produced so many enlightened and honourable men for public service – will most significantly weaken the war against poverty, which required, and still requires, for its successful waging precisely the kind of enlightened, honourable public servants an increasingly classless society does not produce.

Conventional wisdom has it that getting rid of the last lingering remnants of the old hierarchy is a price well worth paying for greater equality of opportunity – that is, for more social, as against economic, equality. This essay seeks to challenge that assumption and to suggest instead that the closer the ideal of everybody having to start from scratch, without even the privileges I enjoyed, is achieved, the greater will be the number who, like me, feel obliged, in large measure, to put their private and domestic responsibilities before their public duties – feel obliged, that is, to feather their own personal nests rather than to concern themselves with the public nest. In other words, the wider we open the gate that gives access to the political class, the fewer there will be who will want to pass through it.

These are the problems this essay will try to address, from the standpoint of an author who was lucky enough in his youth to inherit a place – albeit a very junior one – in the old aristocracy and lucky and ambitious enough in adulthood to win membership, as a newspaper editor, of the new meritocracy; from the standpoint, that is, of someone in a position to make a comparative judgement as to which method of choosing a political class brings the best results. If by 'best' is meant 'the most morally acceptable', the jury is very much still out. For it is by no means certain that the more egalitarian of the two manners of selection is the most popular. Rather the opposite. Far from meritocrats gaining legitimacy more easily than their aristocratic predecessors – as was expected – the opposite seems to be happening. Whereas everybody loved a lord, nobody loves a meritocrat. Possibly this will change. But on present evidence, the possibility has to be faced that democracy and social equality may not be the natural allies they were supposed to be. It could even be that 'the common people' just don't want to be governed by their more successful brothers and sisters.

If, however, 'best' is meant in the sense of serving the nation best, there is only one answer. The trouble is, that those who could bear witness to the superiority of the old aristocracy over the new meritocracy – and their number includes quite as many bottom dogs as top dogs – are now mostly dead, and the few who are still alive feel inhibited by today's egalitarian *Zeitgeist* from doing so. That is the reason for this essay: to break out from the conspiracy of forgetfulness by reminding people that in living memory Britain once had an upper class – from which most of the politicians were drawn – which was the envy of the world. For as a result of this method of selection, Britain's political class had inherited enough in-built authority – honed over three centuries – and enough ancestral wisdom – acquired over the same period – to dare to defy both the arrogance of intellectuals from above and the emotions of the masses from below; to dare to resist the entrepreneurial imperative; to dare to try to raise the level of public conversation; to dare to put the public interest before private interests; and to dare to try to shape the nation's will and curb its appetites. To such a political class conserving the patrimony came naturally, as did the habit of using money to transcend money. Then, most precious asset of all, because its future did not depend wholly on winning votes, Britain's political class could do for demos what courtiers could never do for princes: be a true friend rather than a false flatterer[*]. Also deserving of mention is the elevating effect on British governance generally of its being embedded in an aristocracy through whose park gates could be glimpsed the whole beauty and charm of English history, and the civilizing effect of having a long-established model of high life – celebrated and chronicled by great writers, from Shakespeare to Evelyn Waugh, and portrayed by great painters of every age – that all classes could aspire to share, at least in their dreams. After a visit to the great historian G. M. Trevelyan's older brother, Sir Charles Trevelyan,[†] at Wallington, the family home in Northumberland, A. L. Rowse – himself a distinguished historian from a working-class Cornish background – confided to his diary that the house 'gave him the feeling of how fascinating it would be to belong to a family like that, rich in interest, intelligence, history'.[‡] Many thousands of National Trust members who visit stately homes today will be able to identify with this fascination; a fascination that does not spring from envy but from

---

[*] Nobody has written more eloquently on this theme than Nelson W. Aldrich in *Old Money: Mythology of America's Upper Class* published by Knopf, 1988.

[†] Charles Trevelyan was a socialist who once suggested a general strike to Ernest Bevin, who is said to have replied: 'OK Charlie, I'll bring out the dockers and you bring out the Lord Lieutenants.'

[‡] Quoted in a review by Stefan Collini of *The Diaries of A. L. Rowse*, *Times Literary Supplement* (23 May 2003).

a genuine pride in the existence of such houses and such families.

How can a meritocracy, the political elite of which is likely to change with every generation and to have nothing in common except a shared ability to climb to the top of one of the various ladders of upward mobility, ever hope to enjoy comparable authority? By comparison with the old aristocracy, it is almost bound – unless and until it has had time to develop an authoritative aura of its own – to seem grey, formless, fissiparous, and messy, without colour or character, which is precisely how, starting with C. P. Snow's series of novels in the 1950s and 1960s, it has gone on being portrayed in countless other novels and TV series ever since.[*]

Over thirty years ago, President Kennedy looked forward in a speech[†] to 'a world that will not only be safe for democracy and diversity but also for *distinction*' (my italics). I like to think – having known him a bit – that what he would have wished to say, had his courage extended that far, was that he looked forward to a world that would be safe not only for democracy and diversity but also for 'aristocracy', since, as I try to show in a later chapter, President Kennedy, more than any of his predecessors in the White House, as

---

[*] In his *Strangers and Brothers* sequence, which includes the two best known novels, *The Conscience of the Rich* (1958) and *Corridors of Power* (1964) C. P. Snow shows himself to have been even more enthralled to the old aristocracy, and even more aware of the inadequacies of 'the new men', than was Evelyn Waugh.

[†] Quoted in George Walden's *The New Elites: Making a Career in the Masses* (Allen Lane, 2000).

much in his style as in his rhetoric, set out quite consciously to give at least an aristocratic appearance to America's democratic leadership – just at the very time in the 1960s when the 'angry' movement to eliminate aristocracy – 'that poisonous virus' – from the British body politic began to gain serious momentum.

Two

The English aristocracy is perhaps the most liberal that has ever existed, and no body of men has ever, uninterruptedly, furnished so many honourable and enlightened individuals to the government of a country.

Alexis de Tocqueville, *Democracy in America*, volume i

Thus our democracy was, from an early period, the most aristocratic, and our aristocracy the most democratic in the world.

Macaulay

I, at least, would rather have been governed by Lord Shaftesbury than Mr Cobden, by the gentlemen of England than by the Gradgrinds or Bounderbys of Coketown. There was something picturesque about his thick headiness, something monumental about his complacency. Compare him with the elegant trifler who was the gentleman of the *ancien regime*, or the rigid disciplinarian whom the German aristocracy provided, and he shines in comparison. He was often capable of a generous gesture. He was frequently tolerant, there could be about him a fine quixotism which was difficult not to admire. He threw up odd men of genius like Byron and Henry Cavendish, statesmen of public spirit like Lord John Russell and Hartington; he would found great galleries and establish the British Museum. He was very costly, and, in the mass depressing and dull. Yet, through it all, he always had the saving grace of a sense of humour ... Nor is it certain that we shall replace him by a more admirable type ... The gentleman scourged us with whips. We must beware lest our new masters drive us to our toil with scorpions.

Harold J. Laski, the famously left wing Professor of Politics at the London School of Economics, in his *The Dangers of Being a Gentleman*, Basis Books, 1940

This essay will show: (1) why the aristocratic tradition peculiar to Britain, owing more to manners than to law, more to a religion of good behaviour than to any ideology, and most of all to a particular set of aristocrats at a particular moment in English history, is integral to the spirit of our English constitution; and (2) how getting rid of that tradition is not going to be at all like unburdening the body politic of a heavy handicap, and therefore facilitating its progress into the new millennium, but much more akin to the extraction of an essential organ without which it can no longer healthily survive: as potentially divisive and anarchic in its consequences as was France's violent liquidation of its aristocracy in 1789, from which she did not recover balance and cohesion until Charles de Gaulle, after two empires, three revolutions and four republics, reunited the nation and restored its sanity in 1945, over a century and a half later.

A generation ago, such alarmism would have seemed absurdly pessimistic. Shortly after the last war my old tutor, Herbert Butterfield, the distinguished historian, published a little book called *The Englishman and his History*, in which he wrote: 'When the aristocracy were sent to the laundry the dye ran out into the rest of the washing,' by which he meant that the aristocratic tradition could be, and indeed so far had been, faithfully transferred to and absorbed by the natural aristocrats without pedigrees rising from below. This was true at the time of writing. Even Old Labour seemed quite happy – or at least resigned – to conform to this tradition. A passage in Aneurin Bevan's* fine autobiography is very revealing in this respect. As a radical young miner in a South Wales colliery between the wars 'his concern', he wrote, 'was with one practical question: where does power lie in this particular state of Britain? And how can it be attained by the workers?' His answer was 'Parliament: a sword pointed at the heart of property'.

In theory Bevan was right. Parliament could indeed act as a sword pointed at the heart of property. For Parliament unquestionably does have absolute power; more power than might be dreamt of by a totalitarian dictator – everything short, as some wag put it, 'of the power to turn man into woman', and even that limitation may soon be overcome. But in practice, this omnipotent institution, because the men operating it were either born into or had become part of an aristocracy whose conventions, manners, proprieties, and, above all, comforts discouraged – like all confident aristocracies – any ruthless use of centralized power, almost never did show cold steel, at least in peacetime, as Bevan

---

* *In Place of Fear* (1952).

soon discovered when he actually became an MP and encountered for himself the true spirit of the House of Commons. At first he thought he was in church:

> The vaulted roofs and stained-glass windows, the rows of statues of great statesmen of the past, the echoing halls, the soft-footed attendants and the whispered conversation, contrast depressingly with the crowded meetings and the clang and clash of hot opinions he has just left behind in his election campaign. Here he is, a tribune of the people, coming to make his voice heard in the seats of power. Instead, it seems he is expected to worship; and the most conservative of all religions – ancestor worship.

The 'clang and clash' of opinion; too much of that was indeed what the spirit of the constitution was designed to avoid, and has succeeded in avoiding, give or take a few tense moments, for more than three hundred years. As for ancestor worship, Bevan was spot-on: the spirit of our constitution most certainly does involve ancestor worship, and very rightly so. Even Bevan, in his own idiosyncratic way, paid these ancestors the supreme compliment of emulation by eventually transforming himself, as Jonathan Rose tells us in *The Intellectual Life of the British Working Classes*, into 'a natural aristocrat' who came to suspect that democracy would eventually destroy 'legitimate [as well as illegitimate] superiority'. I remember, as a young journalist, in an interview with Bevan in the late 1950s over a tankard of champagne at the Café Royal, telling him that he was the simulacrum of Charles James Fox, one of the greatest of all of the eighteenth-century Whig grandees. His reaction was to grin from ear to ear, not even demurring when I went on to quote W. H. Mallock's dictum that 'only through aristocracy does a civilized democracy know itself'.

The trouble is that today's political generation, as much among the ranks of the New Conservatives as of the New Labourites, are the first to have had no political education, the history of English statecraft having been eliminated from the curriculum on the grounds of its being too elitist, too much about top dogs who give the orders and not enough about bottom dogs who receive them. So our new rulers know only social history, which concentrates either on class, ethnicity, family, women, children, or universal history and/ or local history:* none of the kinds of history, that is, likely to inspire the best and brightest of the current generation to walk in the footsteps of Chatham, Palmerston, Canning, Disraeli, Gladstone, and all the other parliamentary giants, most of whom they will never have heard of except through entertainment-level TV history, or TV programmes like *Reputations* specifically intended to knock these idols off their pedestals and expose their feet of clay.

What a change from former times. For nearly half a millennium the dream of English youth of the political class

---

* For a profound essay on this subject I would recommend *The New History and the Old* by Gertrude Himmelfarb (Cambridge, Mass.: Harvard University Press/London: Belknap Press, 1987).

was fixed and focused on the House of Commons – 'a modified, socialized arena for battle, drive and dominion', as Sir Lewis Namier put it. Now, however, that story, which used to make a career in Parliament or in public life the highest dream of every schoolboy worth his salt, has been largely erased from memory. When Robin Day, a contemporary of mine, died recently, the obituarists could not understand why his successful life on screen had been no consolation for his failure to get into Parliament. In their eyes, to be a TV inquisitor was by far the more glamorous and envied vocation. And so indeed it has become, which is why Jeremy Paxman can get away with assuming all politicians from the start to be guilty rather than innocent, to be dishonourable rather than honourable gentlemen. How could it be otherwise? For without a knowledge of political history MPs are indeed like the rest of us – deserving of ridicule and censure. Only to those with a knowledge of English political history do they become larger than life figures: not because of their individual merit – by no means always conspicuous – but because of the impressive history of the office they hold.

As for the hereditary members of the House of Lords, their fate is worst of all, since not only is the current generation ignorant of their history but also of the very principles on which their authority rested. This no-go area in public knowledge and imagination leaves a deplorable gap in public debate. For whether we like it or not, the English aristocracy most certainly did play an essential role in forging and shaping Britain's parliamentary institutions, and indeed in shaping almost all our great national institutions, including the Labour Party; so central a role that the venerable traditions they established have long survived the dissolution of the wealth, power, and status of the dukes, earls, and lords who originally called them forth; so central a role that those politicians who now want, using a new detergent called modernization, to rub out once and for all every trace of the true-blue dye, will find it difficult to do so without unravelling – pursuing Butterfield's metaphor – 'the historic garment itself'.

Here, let me make use of Michael Oakeshott's historical abridgement[*], which first brought home to me the unique role played by aristocracy in the development of England's parliamentary government. Oakeshott tells the story of how

---

[*] I owe this abridgement – which I have abridged even further – to an essay entitled 'The Masses in Representative Democracy' published by Michael Oakeshott in 1961. But I can claim to have had a hand in its composition since in 1944 Captain M. J. Oakeshott, as he then was, and Lieutenant P. Worsthorne, as I then was, found ourselves sharing a tent as comrades in arms under canvas waiting, for over a month, to cross the Rhine into Germany. Oakeshott, in civilian life, was already a well-known political philosopher, but at the time I knew nothing of this, and, having recently come down myself from reading history at Cambridge, felt in a position to argue with my superior officer on equal terms. In those days officers had to instil their men in civics, and because several of our fellow officers were Marxists, Oakeshott and I spent many jolly evenings developing this abridgement of the way of offering them an alternative interpretation of modern history. Whether the men were impressed I have no idea – judging by the outcome of the 1945 election, probably not – but that month spent in close communion with Oakeshott, who went on to become one of Britain's most distinguished political philosophers in the last half of the twentieth century, left a lasting impression on me.

towards the end of the Middle Ages there emerged, most spectacularly in Italy, a new kind of human being, the autonomous individual who wanted to be a figure in his own right rather than just an anonymous member of one of the many feudal groups – family, guild, village, church, etc. Such powerful and confident spirits, determined to distance themselves and stand out from their own kind, could be found at all social levels, as much at Court as in the counting house and as much in the hovel as in the baronial hall. For the first time on the human stage appeared Jacob Burckhardt's* *Uomo Unico,* the man who, in the mastery of his circumstances, stood alone and was a law unto himself. Indeed by the middle of the sixteenth century such personalities had been so firmly established that they were beyond the range of mere suppression: not all of the severity of the Calvinist regime in Geneva, for example, was sufficient to quell the impulse to think and behave as an independent individual. The disposition to regard a high degree of individuality in conduct and in belief as the proper condition of mankind, and as the main ingredient of human happiness, had become one of the significant dispositions of modern European character, imposing itself upon art, upon religion, upon morality, upon industry and trade, and upon every kind of human relationship, from husband and wife to ruler and subject.

Naturally, one of the first demands of those intent upon exploring the intimations of individuality was for new

---

* *The Civilization of the Renaissance in Italy* (Part ii).

instruments of government that would allow them to carry on with such explorations without too much let or hindrance; for instruments of government suitable for a society understood as an association of individuals, the prime purpose of which was to seek the most practical adjustments for the avoidance of collision between individuals. A new manner of governing and of being governed appropriate to individuals appeared first in England, in the Netherlands, and in Switzerland, and was later (in various idioms) extended to other parts of Western Europe and the United States. It came to be called parliamentary government.

So much for one side of the coin. But inevitably there was another side as well since the very concatenation of circumstances that produced the Renaissance man – an individual determined to escape from the ties of feudal community – also produced the anti-individual anxious to go on enjoying the protection of these communal ties. And this counter-disposition, which perceived the throwing-off of the ties of community more as a threat than a liberation, was also to be found in all ranks of society, very much including the nobility since for every baron or general who wanted to take the risk of climbing onto a white horse to seize a crown, there were many others who were happy to carry on enjoying the feudal privileges they already enjoyed. So anti-individuals came in all shapes and sizes – a lack of strength and confidence being as common among the rich as the poor, and from the beginning of the sixteenth century they too, in turn, gathered to themselves their own distinctive understanding of an appropriate manner of government and of being governed: one that cast government in the role of architect and custodian, not of 'public *order*' in an association of individuals pursuing their own activities, but rather of 'the public *good*' as a community. They wanted a ruler who was not to be the referee of the collisions of individuals, but the moral leader and managing director of 'the community'. And if we call the manner of government generated by the aspirations of individuality 'parliamentary government', then, Oakeshott goes on to argue, we may call the modification of it under the impact of the mass man, 'populist government'. And it is important to understand that these are two wholly different manners of government.

In short, the circumstances of modern Europe, even as early as the sixteenth century, bred not a single character, but two obliquely opposed characters: not only the individual but the individual *manqué*. And the individual *manqué* was no more a relic of the feudal age than the individual himself since both were essentially modern characters – with no equivalence in the ancient world: both were products of the same dissolution of the old feudal ties.

It is not enough, therefore, to say that the emergence of the individual was the pre-eminent event in modern history, for although that is true, it is not the whole truth. For the emergence of the anti-individual, or individual *manqué*, happened almost simultaneously – the one being merely the shadow and the other the substance – and if the individual gathered to himself one understanding of government and one set of political manners, of a kind likely to maximize individual freedom, the anti-individual gathered to himself another understanding of government and another form of political manners of a kind likely to maximize collective security. So as early as the sixteenth century the governments of Europe were being remade, not only in response to the demands of individuality, but also in response to the needs of the individual *manqué*, the 'godly prince' of the Reformation and his lineal descendant, the enlightened despot of the eighteenth century, these being political inventions for making choices for those indisposed to make choices for themselves, just as parliamentary democracy was the political invention of individuals confident and powerful enough not to have to assume that the State will always defeat them in the end.

The story of the conflict between these two dispositions, which has been continuing ever since, is exceedingly complex, with most European countries swinging to and fro between the two. But what concerns me here, as I say, is the unique role played by the English aristocracy in resolving that conflict in favour of the instruments of parliamentary government – the instruments appropriate to individuality – and, what is more, resolving the conflict so decisively that, so far, there has been no serious attempt to reopen it.

For four decades before 1688, England had suffered from various attempts to meet the needs of the individual *manqué*: first, under the Stuarts, through a romantic-sounding return to monarchical absolutism, and then – the tail-side of the same individual *manqué* coin – through assorted outbursts (Diggers and Fifth Monarchists, Levellers and Ranters) of populist idealism. All sorts of Utopian experiments aimed at creating a political system responsive to the individual *manqué* – ranging from the abolition of the House of Lords to disestablishment of the Church of England, from military dictatorship to a written constitution, from primitive communism to a fully democratic society – were tried and found horribly wanting, if only because all of them were soon seen to threaten, in one way or the other, that post-feudal condition of human circumstances that had come to be known as individual freedom. Instead of continuing that steady abrogation of feudal privilege that in England had granted all individuals, regardless of rank, freedom of movement, speech, belief and religious observance, association and disassociation, of bequest and inheritance, and the right to be ruled by a known law, applicable to all subjects alike, these forays into populist Utopianism and monarchical absolutism had turned the tide in the opposite direction – in the direction of a society fit only for anti-individuals to live in.

Here, I think, we come to the crux. For it was at this low point for individuals, induced by the Civil War horrors, that there began to emerge a new and peculiarly English modification of the ideal autonomous individual; an understanding rooted in a new awareness that while *Uomo Unico*, who was a law unto himself, had certainly been necessary to enable individuals to break out of the bonds of feudalism, a rather more civilized understanding of individuality had to be engendered to meet the new challenge of avoiding collision in a society made up of individuals; an understanding of individuality appropriate to parliamentary rulers rather than for condottieri princes. Yes, each individual had a natural right to make his own choices, to be captain of his own soul and master of his fate; but unless that right was exercised in moderation, then horrible collisions would be unavoidable, as England's recent suffering had bloodily demonstrated. So the ideal of individuality required to be subtly modified if parliamentary government was to work. Instead of being the Renaissance Man, overweeningly confident of his power to govern others, the individual must become a *gentle man*, confident of his power to govern himself, since only someone possessed of such confidence – able to mind his own business – would be unlikely to feel a compulsion to dominate others – to mind other people's business. In other words, for a free society to remain orderly what was needed, as much among rulers as among ruled, was the *civilized* individual with an inbred inclination towards compromise, accommodation, and reconciliation. Of course it was understood that individuals needed, and benefited from, strong government; but only in a society made up of *self*-governing individuals would rulers be strong without being oppressive and the ruled consensual without being submissive.

By the seventeenth century, English individuals with this new understanding were soon to be found in all walks of life, but aristocrats, being then the most powerful group in the land, were the only ones in a position to put them into practice. Thus in England it was a group of aristocratic individuals, rather than a group of bourgeois individuals, or a group of proletarian individuals, who, with miraculous bloodlessness, carried out the Glorious Revolution of 1688 – glorious because, by putting to rights the botched job perpetrated by the regicides who cut off King Charles's head, it solved the problem of monarchical absolutism in such a way as to produce lasting settlement rather than future tumult. No other aristocrats in history have had anything comparable to their credit. In France's case, the job was left to the bourgeoisie, who, like their English counterparts more than a century earlier, made a bloody mess of it, as did the Russian workers – or at any rate the leaders of the Bolshevik Party – in 1917. Only English aristocrats did the job successfully, stabilizing – at least vestigially through the House of Lords – social control and political power in the descendants of that particular aristocracy.

So not only was England's aristocracy unique in solving the problems of monarchical absolutism; it was also unique, as a consequence, in being able to shape parliamentary institutions in its own particular image. For only in England was a revolutionary settlement that established forms of government suitable for an association of individuals reached long before – indeed a whole century before – the individual *manqué* had discovered that, far from being alone, he was in fact one of many; had discovered, in short, that his strength lay in superior numbers. Equally important, England's parliamentary institutions were in place well before a certain perverse type of individual, the populist demagogue, had discovered the joys of exercising his own individuality by putting himself at the head and offering to

lead the other individuals *manqué*. For almost by definition
the individual *manqué* needs to be told what to think, his
impulses have to be transformed into desires, and those
desires into projects; he has to be made aware of his power,
and those were the tasks of a leader. In the seventeenth
century, however, his leaders were still mostly politically
unsophisticated visionaries, only dimly aware of their purpose and lacking a large audience. Moreover, many of them
were royalists and Cavalier aristocrats (Jacobites) using a
communitarian vocabulary that was profoundly confusing,
since it relied quite as much on backward-looking notions
of hierarchy and status as on forward-looking notions of
equality and solidarity. In other words, England's revolutionary settlement, which assured the future of parliamentary government, was uniquely lucky in its timing since it
came so very long before the whole Marx–Engels idea of
'the masses' – with a morality of their own which must be
imposed on everybody else – had yet been adumbrated.
Thus it was that by the late nineteenth century, when it *had*
been adumbrated, Herbert Butterfield's 'true-blue dye' had
penetrated so deeply into England's constitutional arrangements as to be uniquely hard to erase. Thus, unlike the
parliamentary systems of all the other major European countries, Britain's had had time to develop a body politic – of
which the aristocracy was a crucial part – strong enough to
resist the political poison which, in the twentieth century,
carried off most of all the other bodies politic.

In any case, to begin with, few Englishmen wanted to
erase that true-blue dye, because only in England had aristo-

cratic individuality been civilized. Besides, mindful of the Stuart and Cromwellian tyrannies, and the equally destructive outbursts of populist idealism, nobody wanted to risk a return to transformational politics. Accommodation, reconciliation, compromise, an inclination to let sleeping dogs lie and not to frighten the horses – these were the mild and gentle influences shaping the spirit of the new settlement:– influences almost beyond the comprehension of the legal mind.

Hence the inevitability of letting the non-controversial spirit grow, not out of doctrine but out of actions, the first example of which was the Whig success in persuading the Tory–Jacobite dissidents to return to the fold. After that was achieved – by the defeat of the Young Pretender in 1745 – the reunited aristocracy never disagreed again on what A. P. Thornton, in his great classic *The Habit of Authority: Paternalism in British History**, calls 'the fundamentals'; never disagreed again, that is, on the fundamental importance of preventing abstract principles being turned into aggressive weapons to the point where civil strife ensued. Insofar as this country could be said to have a social contract, that was it: an unwritten agreement by all sections of the aristocracy to exercise power in what came to be known as a 'gentlemanly' manner; an unwritten agreement which, having succeeded in transforming the barren divides between Whigs and Tories, church and chapel, into a fruitful

---

* I was enthralled by this work when it was published by George Allen & Unwin in 1966, and have drawn wisdom from it ever since.

cleavage, went on to do the same, in later centuries, for liberalism and conservatism and finally, most triumphantly of all, for socialism and capitalism.

That is why in our Parliament there came to be such a term as unparliamentary language – unmannerly language, unbefitting of an assembly of honourable gentlemen. Unparliamentary language is unparliamentary not because it is hostile or insulting to the member or members to whom it is addressed, but because it is insulting to the fundamental purpose of Parliament, which is to find a way to avoid ill will and confrontation. Hence, for example, the civilized convention that there should be no legislation so controversial as to prevent government ministers, after all the ding-dong in the Chamber of the House of Commons, 'from dining with the Opposition'. In England, manners (or rather civility) makyth man, not only socially but politically as well. The secret of the British system of government is thus to have a distinct political class that can afford to disagree fiercely about goals because it agrees so firmly with the rules to be followed in pursuing those goals.

So it needs to be remembered that the English people's love of a lord went much deeper than mere snobbery. For the success of the Glorious Revolution was not due to political science; it was due to the practical political skills displayed by certain aristocratic families who won for themselves, and for their descendants, a degree of gratitude from the governed that no other aristocracy in history has ever enjoyed, or deserved to enjoy. So it was not to aristocracy in principle but to a particular aristocracy in practice that the English people gave their trust. Initially it must have seemed the merest commonsense to do so – at any rate until the winning formula had become so much a general habit as to have developed a natural momentum of its own. Of course a written constitution would have made sense if the aim had been to preserve the fruits of a successful revolution that had followed a logical blueprint. But to preserve the fruits of a successful revolution, like the Glorious Revolution, that had followed no logical blueprint, it made more sense to hang on for dear life to the aristocratic descendants of the revolutionaries themselves, in the hope that something of their ancestors' amazingly successful governing style might have rubbed off on them – a hope which, in the event, turned out to have been well justified.

So England's aristocracy became the buttress not only of English liberties but also of local autonomy against centralized bureaucracy, in such marked contrast with what was happening in the seventeenth century in France, where Louis XIV was turning his aristocracy into the buttress of a centralized and all-powerful State.

This was the time, it also needs to be remembered, when English nationalism had just got into its stride as the be-all and end-all of reality, and in the light of that reality a likeminded, closely-bonded upper class, supplying the personnel for both Opposition and Government and occupying all the high offices of Church and State, was obviously a good way to ensure the all-important purpose of effective government, particularly when the upper class in question, precisely because of the growth of mutual trust within its ranks, began to show not only an unprecedented willingness to embrace upwardly mobile meritocrats, but also to tolerate dissent. Certainly, even then, the aristocracy had its egalitarian enemies who argued that it was unfair because it favoured a minority of individuals at the expense of the majority. But even enemies of aristocracy could hardly question the counter assertion that aristocracy was a system favouring the nation. For under aristocratic governance the nation was going from strength to strength. Moreover, aristocratic rule in England bore no resemblance to the kinds of despotic power that modern science seemed to be unleashing for the use of Hobbes's Leviathan. Instead it took the form of domesticated and civilized power – power consisting of multiple accommodations and understandings; power refined by customs and traditions; power grounded in history rather than in raw rationality; and above all, power exercised by English noblemen who were even then in the process of being transformed into English gentlemen.

So English aristocracy is best understood as a particular manner of exercising power – a uniquely domesticated and civilized manner of exercising power, which in turn encouraged and made possible an equally civilized manner of exercising powerlessness. No more than the former could adequately be described as merely courtly good manners or courtesy, could the latter be adequately described as mere deference or subservience, since both sprang from a shared moral commitment by the best in all classes to put the good of the whole society before their own interests or the interests of their class. What I am describing is known as civility: a state of mind that makes enough among the governing classes and enough among the governed classes consciously wish to develop sufficient trust between each other to prevent conflict boiling over into violence. Civility, as my friend the late Professor Edward Shils has argued in many books and papers, is what makes enough among the governing and governed classes believe in supporting the governmental institutions that lay down the rules for resolving conflict; and enough among the powerless and the powerful to constitute a consensus when it comes to maintaining order in society. Old-fashioned courtesy, of course, is a part of civility, since good manners ameliorate the strain that accompanies the risks and dangers, the losses and injuries, of an economically, politically, and intellectually competitive society in which some people are bound to lose; but it is only the outward manifestation of the true deep spirit of civility, which lies in a moral commitment to understand your opponent's prejudices rather than to expose his errors, to accommodation rather than confrontation.

It could and has been argued that civility is merely a ruse by which the powerful con the powerless into accepting an unjust status quo. For civility does indeed preclude political radicalism of the kind concerned with the gratification of the individual at the expense of the public good. So civility most certainly does put brakes on the exercise of individual civil rights – or rather on the exercise of civil rights to the point where the public good is threatened, from which it might be inferred that it is a force on the side of the powerful. But against that it has to be emphasized that civility most definitely also puts brakes on any abuse of power that leaves the powerless with no alternative but to pull the pillars down. In other words, there is a civility that civilizes the ruthless antisocial tendencies inherent in the exercise of power, just as there is a civility – the reverse side of the coin – that civilizes the ruthless antisocial Jacobinical tendencies inherent in powerlessness. Tolerant and genial paternalism, on the one side, and tolerant and genial subordination – not to be confused with servility or forelock pulling – on the other, these two habits in combination constitute the spirit of England's unwritten constitution, the seeds of which were sown by the aristocratic revolutionaries of 1688 and have been flowering ever since, as European visitors, starting with Voltaire in the eighteenth century and followed by De Tocqueville, Taine, and many others in the nineteenth and twentieth centuries, have often enviously noted. Indeed, only the French Jacobins of the 1790s took a more jaundiced view, rightly maintaining that 'no other revolutionary government could ever build its institutions on England's tolerant habits'. Those habits, I would argue, were essentially aristocratic habits since of all systems of government, aristocracy – or at least England's civilised version of aristocracy – is the most likely to encourage a society to appreciate, in the words of Michael Oakeshott, 'that the greater part of what it has is not a burden to be carried or an incubus to be thrown off, but an inheritance to be enjoyed. And a certain degree of shabbiness is joined with every real convenience.'

Precisely so: the combination of inequality and inherited privilege was the inevitable 'shabbiness' to which was joined the 'real convenience' of having a tolerant (always relative to the times, of course) system of government. So much depended on the existence of a political culture that looked at everything, not ideologically but pragmatically. By this token, equality was a good thing theoretically, but if in practice the price of imposing it thoroughly would be to replace an existing lot of tolerant and genial rulers – because established and secure – by a lot of almost certainly insecure and rough-edged rulers, because new and unestablished, that seemed a poor bet; a poor bet because a political culture based on civility would be replaced by a political culture based on incivility. By the same token, the rights and freedoms of ordinary people were also important. But did it not stand to reason that the only way to ensure the civil rights and freedoms of the powerless was first to ensure the civil rights and freedoms of the powerful, since the institutions required to protect the one could not fail, in the end, to do the same, at any rate to some degree, for the other? Furthermore, in defiance of all theoretical assumptions, the English aristocracy had in practice proved quite as much a friend as a foe of freedom and democracy, supplying as many of the leaders of the one cause as of the other. Democracy in theory might mean rule by the common man in the street, but in practice the defeat of tyrants was much better left to the uncommon man. An ideal democrat was a leader who, like St George, slew tyrants, be they evil kings, overmighty subjects, bloody mobs, aggressive foreign dictators or, after the General Strike in 1926, domineering trade union barons. In fact the democratic ideal was so demanding that only true aristocrats could hope to live up to it. What is more, in practice – as against theory – even such a left-wing firebrand as Jenny Lee, Aneurin Bevan's wife and herself a working-class MP, made this assumption, since how else, when staying in a Welsh miner's home, could she have felt justified – as she did – in always putting her shoes outside the bedroom door, automatically assuming some other member of the household would undertake the menial task of cleaning and polishing them? This patrician assumption did not mean that she was not a democrat: it meant that she believed a democratic leader deserved special privileges. In theory, both Aneurin Bevan and Jenny Lee were ardent egalitarians, but what they meant by egalitarianism was greater opportunity for natural aristocrats like themselves to be unequal. For the people, in their view, deserved the finest, noblest leaders – people who had proved their worth – rather than the chinless upper-class idlers who were not true aristocrats at all, any more than were grasping, mean-minded businessmen.*

Therein lay England's peculiarity: aristocracy was the only model for social ambition. For just as in the eighteenth and nineteenth centuries the aspiring bourgeoisie were per-

---

* Woodrow Wyatt's diaries tell us that Bevan's doctor was Sir Dan Davies, doctor to George VI, whom he, of course, consulted privately. Wyatt says that Bevan was a natural aristocrat – the NHS was good enough for everyone else, but not for him.

suaded to take the ideal of aristocracy as their model, so in the twentieth century were the aspiring members of the working class inspired to do likewise. In this, of course, they were only echoing the view of the French Jacobinical revolutionaries of 1789 who were also quite shockingly elitist, demanding far more superiority – far higher levels of loyalty, duty and even purity – of their leaders than anything demanded by France's *ancien régime*. When Mary Wollstonecraft visited Paris during the height of the Terror, she was delighted by their exactingly elitist high standards. Indeed they struck her as more genuinely aristocratic – in the sense of rule by the best – than were the aristocrats of old.* In any case, the very idea that every citizen, even the most politically inactive and self-absorbed, could have a serious say in government appealed no more to arch-radicals than to arch-conservatives, not simply because, in a large complex society, of its impracticality but because it was also undesirable. No serious cause, any more than any serious nation, could be entrusted to direct rule by the people. Down that path would lie decline and chaos. After all, not even Jesus, in whose sight all men were truly equal, believed that everybody could be an apostle, choosing instead only an aristocracy, for heaven's sake, of twelve.

I hope enough has been said to make clear that I am not talking about aristocracy as an exclusive caste limited only to families with enough feudal quarterings to make their

---

* See Claire Tomalin's *The Life and Death of Mary Wollstonecraft* (1974).

blood the purest blue. By 1688 that understanding of aristocracy had long since been undermined by Protestantism, with its emphasis on the central importance of individual conscience, over which no power on earth, not even blue blood, could exercise dominion. In the most important sense of all, therefore, the meanest post-Reformation English citizen had already become sovereign over his own soul, exactly equal, in that fundamental respect, to the grandest in the land. So in England, unlike in Catholic France, the aristocracy was buttressed by no semi-religious legitimizing doctrine – only, as Burke was so loudly to proclaim, by tradition, rooted in experience: by good works rather than by faith. Blessed with an open-ended, easy-going, and gentlemanly governing class, it simply made sense for the English people to stick with nurse for fear of getting something worse. Certainly England's social system could be faulted by some reference to a theoretical rights of man, but its practical record of ensuring that the right kind of man – the gentleman – wielded power and influence was remarkably good. Character is what redeems the dirty work of politics, and character is what the aristocracy produced.

Montesquieu missed the point when he gave credit for England's tradition of individual liberty to our balanced constitution that separated executive, legislative, and judiciary, since in reality the secret of its success lay rather in all three branches of the State being operated by members of the same interlocking ruling class. This, because of a shared commitment to civility – shared, in their fashion, by the ruled classes – enabled the whole society, as befits a genuine body politic, to achieve an almost organic degree of trust and cooperation, which, because of the class system, was passed on from generation to generation. So as Cardinal Newman once wrote: 'It was not only to parks and palaces that the law of entails applies.'

Needless to say, if the English aristocracy had been a rigorously exclusive caste – as it was in France and on the Continent generally – it would not have survived without provoking violent revolutions. It was, however, uniquely porous, the English upper class displaying the same realistically restrained approach to aristocracy as the English lower classes did to democracy. In both cases there was a reluctance to go for broke or to push their luck. Just as there was always room left for a democratic dimension in England's aristocracy, so there was always room left for an aristocratic dimension in English democracy. Thus by the end of the nineteenth century all that was needed to get to the top was enough money to maintain the material standards of a gentleman over one generation and, just as important, the patience to wait for the required graces to grow. In short, it was not all that difficult for the English captains of industry to transfer themselves peacefully into lords of the manor, MPs, or JPs.

Unlike the French bourgeoisie, who had to stage two violent revolutions to gain access to political influence and social status, and in the course of that struggle had no choice but to develop their own separate identity and values (and tenacious organizations to give them effect), our English bourgeoisie, very much in contrast, were quite happy to merge with those of 'their betters', to whom they felt indebted rather than resentful. And a genuine merger it proved to be, with sections of the aristocracy in the nineteenth century accepting quite as many bourgeois virtues and vices – respectability, hypocrisy, the Protestant ethic of hard work, sobriety and thrift, charitable good works – as sections of the bourgeoisie did the aristocratic virtues and vices – loyalty, honour, luxury and idleness. Indeed it was out of this uniquely engaging mix that the ideal of the English gentleman sprang. The emancipation of the bourgeoisie thus served to strengthen rather than weaken the *ancien régime*. No new alternative source of bourgeois authority – let alone grace – was created; the old aristocratic one merely broadened its base.

The English working class, on the other hand, had to fight much harder for their place in the sun, an experience that did produce one tenacious organization, the trade union movement, with its very own culture and hierarchy, and another, the Labour Party, also with a culture and hierarchy very largely of its own. But even those two institutions, thanks to the mild addiction of the English middle class to the mellow spirit of *noblesse oblige*, had an easier ride than their working-class counterparts in France. In this respect it is revealing to compare Matthew Arnold's merely patronizing distain for the philistinism of the English bourgeoisie, as expressed in *Culture and Anarchy*, with Flaubert's implacable hatred for the selfish ruthlessness of their French counterparts, as expressed in his novel *L'Éducation sentimentale*. Toughest of all, in the twentieth century, were

American employers like Henry Ford who – as described by Edmund Wilson – went so far as to hire aircraft to strafe striking workers from the air!

By comparison, the English working class was relatively lucky (though admittedly this isn't saying all that much). For unlike every other bourgeois class, the English variety was unique in including a significant number quite as concerned to become gentlemen – which precluded being seen to have your snout too deeply in the trough – as to become millionaires. Of course greed and acquisitiveness have always played their part in all walks of English life but comparatively seldom, at least until very recently, unapologetically and brazenly. Such behaviour, in the phrase that is so much mocked, simply 'wasn't done'. It took a long time, for example, for the nabobs, returning from making their fortunes in the East India Company, to be received by 'the County'. Not only was the brutal manner in which they had acquired their fortunes held against them (*vide* Burke's determination to impeach Warren Hastings) but so were the provocatively ostentatious palaces they built – now, of course, very much part of England's heritage. Unquestionably there was much hypocrisy in this lofty censoriousness but hypocrisy, as we know, is the tribute vice pays to virtue. 'Happy is the society', as Nadezhda Mandelstam wrote, 'in which despicable behaviour at least has to be disguised'; in that sense, at least, Britain had rather more reasons to be happy in the bad old days than it has now – and this applies as much to sport and the arts as to politics and business.

Writing after the First World War about Victorian England, the great German historian of the period, Dr Dibelius, said that 'All democratic forms notwithstanding, the English gentleman will always rule because he has captured the soul of the people' – a somewhat Germanic way of saying that the English love a lord. He did not go on to say that a combination of *Burke's Peerage* and Debrett had replaced the Bible as Holy Writ, but he came very near to doing so. Of course the gentlemanly ideal took different forms: in the upper class *noblesse oblige*; in the bourgeois middle classes, 'a gentleman's word is as good as his bond', symbolized by the custom of shaking hands after doing a deal; in the working class, the deep instinctive sense of decency and fair play, particularly in sport; and in the universities, or at least at Oxford and Cambridge, a commitment quite as much to nurturing gentlemanly rulers as to producing scholars.

If this is beginning to sound like another elegy for a vanished age of aristocracy, that is only partially intended. Certainly that hierarchical England, by a fortunate accident of birth, suited me personally, easing my life at every adult stage, except – which was part of its purpose – at boarding school; but it is not in the least difficult to imagine the pain and frustration it caused to the unfortunate many whose talents were so cruelly wasted. No words of mine, however, are needed to underline the downside of the class system – the shameful contrast of distress among so much privilege – since that aspect of our history is not at all overlooked by the contemporary media; nor is it overlooked in drama or historical documentaries, which dwell on very little else. The whole contemporary culture is now as much saturated with anti-snobbery as it was once saturated with snobbery, to the point where the virtues of the class system, and the contribution made by it to England's record of political and social stability – from which all classes immeasurably benefited – is largely, if not totally, ignored. For it was our class system, far more than any written constitution, that produced a clear source of political and social authority, so clear and recognizable as to minimize the need for coercion or even for a standing army. (The Royal Navy, unlike the navy of the Tsars, was used only to bombard foreigners.) Indeed it was the middle of the nineteenth century before it was thought necessary to organize a national police force.

Not that this has ever meant any absence of figures endowed with social authority: long before the Peelers, the country abounded in them. Anyone who spoke like a gentleman, dressed like a gentleman, carried himself like a gentleman – pretty well the entire upper, middle, and professional classes – were more than able to overawe, and do so just as authoritatively by carrying a rolled umbrella and wearing a bowler hat as did the boys in blue by wielding truncheons and wearing helmets.

Authority in the armed forces, too, largely came from the same source, greatly easing the problems of discipline, since soldiers instinctively obeyed any officer who was a gentleman – so long as he was brave, which most of them were brought up to be. This was a great advantage to the nation in times of war, providing the armed forces with natural reservoirs of leadership material from which to draw.

Whereas a Prussian Junker had to bark at and bully his men, a British officer could get the same result by scarcely raising his voice; indeed raising his voice was positively counter-productive.

Class attributes also greatly helped the Church of England's bishops and clergy, often ensuring a respect for the cloth that the Word of God on its own would never have vouchsafed. No doubt great saintliness would have been best of all, but since that is always very exceptional, gentlemanliness came in very handy as a satisfactory substitute, as it came in handy, too, as a substitute for military prowess.

The same was true of the judges, whose ability to resist unjust pressure from the State and, just as important, populist and media pressure, either for cruel vengeance or sentimental forgiveness, owed almost as much to their high social status as to their official position. In Marxist theory, of course, the judge's class associations should have had the opposite effect, making them more rather than less responsive to State pressure and less likely to administer justice to the ordinary individual without fear or favour; and in certain respects – in offences against property, like poaching – this was all too often the case. But in the all-important matter of preventing abuse of power by the State, the English judiciary, like the rest of the aristocracy, was often on the side of the libertarian angels, if only because an hereditary aristocracy, with relations extending far beyond the corridors of power into disreputable nooks and crannies on which the law is just as likely to scowl as to smile, had as constant a need for an independent judiciary as did the unprivileged classes; was just as likely, that is, to need their freedoms protected by the common law as any humble family, not because of any high-flown abstract love of civil liberties, but because their own kith and kin had more need than anybody else to make use of these freedoms.

For what is often forgotten is that it takes power to guarantee freedom and justice and the upper-class families who had the power produced more than their fair share of black sheep, eccentrics, nonconformists, iconoclasts, blasphemers and deviants of every shade and variety, none of whom took kindly to being told by the State what not to say or do. So far as Britain was concerned, therefore, the phrase 'ruling class' was somewhat misleading, since the ruling class supplied quite as many libertarians, like Charles James Fox, as it did authoritarian rulers, like William Pitt. As a result, the authority springing from class served not only to facilitate a worrying degree of illiberal exercise of power but also, reassuringly, a countervailing liberal exercise of resistance to power, whether of the State, or of capital, or of public opinion, or of all three acting in concert. As Disraeli said, the Chartists might have won if they'd had the good sense to choose an aristocrat to lead them.[*]

In theory, of course, it should be quite the other way round. A participatory, classless democracy should be a much better buttress of individual liberty than a class system. On this point, however, even Tocqueville, in *Democracy in America*, had some practical doubts: 'In democratic

---

[*] See Disraeli's novel *Sybil* (1845).

times . . .', he wrote, 'the bond of affection is extended, but it is also relaxed', by which he meant that a large nation of equals may in theory all love each other tenderly, but in practice their bonds of affection will be far too impersonal ever to form a concentration of power able to withstand the concentrated power of the State, particularly when the State has the winds of public opinion in its sails. In a meritocracy, the bonds are likely to be even looser, since meritocrats, each having climbed up the ladder alone – which is the only way to climb a ladder – are the last people likely to put civility before self-advancement.

Aristocracy, however, is different because the bonds, forged at birth and maintained at every subsequent stage in life, create a degree of loyalty between members as strong as, if not stronger than, those that bind together the members of a nation. The Old Etonian George Orwell tried to escape them but never wholly succeeded, concluding sadly, at the end of his life, that it was easier to change your party than to change your class. Speaking personally, I cannot imagine life without class, which is not a passive condition but one that provides you with a general culture, a network to which you naturally belong, a stream of history in which you feel free and safe – almost a collective individuality. Much the same was true of the hereditary working class, which also, as a result of the extraordinary, almost mystical solidarity engendered, was able for a time, through the trade unions, to bring the State to its knees. But in a classless society, without those involuntary civil associations with their uniquely cohesive strength, where will the resistance to the State come from? From all the equal citizens acting together is the aspirational answer, which provokes comment, this time in the words not of Tocqueville, but of the great Duke of Wellington, replying to a stranger who had addressed him in St James's Street as Mr Smith: 'If you can believe that, sir, you can believe anything.' As for the media, protection from that tainted source, we are beginning to realize, amounts to falling out of the frying pan into the fire.

In short, class, until recently, was what kept the liberal, quite as much as the conservative, show on the road. By this, let me repeat, I do not mean dukes and earls and lords, but rather the institutions on which the old ruling class put its stamp: Parliament, the Church of England, Oxbridge, the public schools, the Civil Service, the MCC, the London clubs, the armed forces, the City of London, the judiciary, the professions, even the old Labour Party itself and the trade unions. Increasingly in the nineteenth and twentieth centuries, those passing through these institutions in their youth, or serving in them in their adult lives, were meritocrats; but so all-embracing were the rites of passage that they too acquired the aristocratic 'public philosophy', and a sense of responsible imperium along with the appropriate habits of authority, manners, accent, and dress code. Anybody, as I say, with brains and ambitions could join the club, the only condition being that they should be willing to behave civilly, as pretty well all the old top echelon of Old Labour – many of whom ended up in the House of Lords – manifestly did.

What we used to have, therefore, was a social system, the last remnants of which are now being eradicated, that made it easy for our political institutions to mobilize enough consent to govern effectively without coercion. For the most part, the politicians did not need to be, like Lloyd George, political virtuosos* – who, apart from being dangerous, are inevitably in short supply – because the right class attributes were enough to endow non-high-flyers with authority. So even mediocre government – except in emergencies – sufficed, and this enabled the body politic, as Adam Smith observed, to survive 'a deal of ruin'. Public expectations were never so unrealistic as to be bound to be disappointed. Governments were given the benefit of the doubt. Instead of having to please individuals or small groups, all with their conflicting agendas, governments had to please cohesive classes, a much more manageable proposition. Few governments, in reality, deserve trust, at least not for long. Examined with a suspicious eye, hidden defects are bound to appear. The same goes for the governed, to whose notorious selfishness and fickleness a blind eye also needs to be turned. So trust, on both sides has to be habitual to the point of instinctive, with roots – put down over generations – deep enough to survive all the natural squalls of press and public scepticism. The governed, to a degree which now seems incomprehensible, had indeed got into the habit of trusting the ruling class, and the ruling class, more than any other

---

* See J. H. Grainger, *Character and Style in English Politics* (1969). This is another excellent work to which I owe a great debt.

similar class in Europe, had indeed got into the habit of trusting the people, both believing as a matter of faith that to do so was in the kingdom's widest interest. Duty also came into it: duty on the part of the governed to trust the governors, and duty on the part of the governors not to abuse that trust. This was a compact, the value of which was again proved during the 1920s and 1930s when the temptations of communism in the lower classes, and fascism in the upper, were successfully resisted.

Harold Laski, Professor of Politics at the LSE, writing in the 1930s at the depth of the Depression, was convinced that, because the upper classes were planning to breach the constitution in a fascistic defence of property, the lower classes would be justified in pre-empting that coup by an equally unconstitutional communistic attack on property. The evidence he gave for the existence of this fascistic threat was that the Conservative party of the day, by exploiting its influence over the press, the cinema, the theatre, and the Church of England, was trying to strengthen the power of the Lords and the prestige of the monarchy and the class system generally. Given the current crisis of capitalism, he argued, the historic constitutional compact between the classes was bound to give way to dictatorship, as it was doing in the rest of Europe. In the event, of course, the very snobbery Laski saw as likely to facilitate fascism in England did the opposite, since it was Sir Oswald Mosley's ungentlemanly strut, ungentlemanly black shirt and boots, hate-soaked rhetoric, and ungentlemanly love of brutal violence that rendered fascism un-English in the eyes of all classes.* No written constitution would have been nearly so effective. What stopped fascism in its tracks in England was not so much its threat to freedom as its threat to civility, as Laski eventually came to recognize when he wrote: 'The gentlemen of England scourged us with whips; we must beware that the new men do not scourge us with scorpions.'

Nor did the compact falter in the Second World War, or in the years of Old Labour's rule from 1945 to 1951, when the socialist government of the day relied greatly on the old governing class (rather more on Wykehamists than Old Etonians) to run the welfare state, or in the withdrawal from empire, which, apart from the Suez bruise, left few scars on the British body politic – unlike France whose imperial retrenchment produced bloodletting so great that it killed off the Fourth Republic. As for the Cold War years, Britain's body politic also took that strain with remarkable coolness, never allowing anti-communist hysteria to endanger civil liberties, unlike in the USA where McCarthyism, supported by the Republican Party, ran wildly out of control. The treason threat was certainly no greater in America than here, arguably rather less. Indeed, with what we now know of the English spy rings' closeness to the very centres of power, the threat was probably greater here than there. So why the difference in the quality of the reactions? The answer given by the distinguished American historian Richard Hofstadter is very clear: while Britain had a ruling class with enough

* See P. G. Wodehouse's character Roderick Spode, based on Mosley, in *The Code of the Woosters* (1938).

'political and moral autonomy' to defy 'the wildest currents of public sentiment', the United States did not; and when push came to shove, the English Establishment provided a more effective protection to civil liberties than did America's written constitution.

Where England's *ancien régime* did falter, of course, was on the post-war economic front in the 1950s, 1960s, and 1970s. But this, it could be argued, was because of its virtues rather than its vices; its sensitivity rather than its callousness. I once asked Harold Macmillan, then a very old man, why the post-war Conservative governments managed the economy so badly during those years. His defence of 'wetness' went something like this. 'It was a case', he said, 'of putting statesmanship before economic management. After its sacrifices during the war, and before the war in the slump, the British nation deserved a decade or two of living beyond its means; had won for itself the right to loosen its belt. In the language of economics', he went on, 'this spelt inflation. But in the language of statesmanship it meant sparing the camel the last straw which might break its back.' That was the way they spoke in those pre-Thatcher days.

Not a bad record, I would have thought, for an *ancien régime* now being consigned to the dustheap of history. Truth to tell, the most unanswerable case left-wing critics can make is that it worked too well, thereby making life intolerably difficult for revolutionaries – an unforgivable sin if you are a revolutionary. Not enough went wrong. The governing class made concessions too easily, were too accommodating, too gentle; denying the people their fair share, not so much of bread and freedom, as of *grievances* – in particular, the grievance of blocking upward social mobility that had obligingly produced so many revolutions on the Continent.

So while the British have had three centuries' experience of a particular kind of parliamentary democracy – one inlaid by aristocracy and topped by the Crown – ruling successfully over a socially stratified society, they can have no idea yet if this same democracy can rise to the challenge of governing a socially unstratified, classless society, to the achievement of which all three of the major political parties are, at least in theory, now committed.

Three

Poor fucking novelists in a classless Britain.

Kingsley Amis

"Class is class, I saw it then, the English Gentleman . . . you cannot beat it, you cannot say you know England until you know the English Gentleman."

Letter from Angela to the narrator in V. S. Naipaul's novel, *The Enigma of Arrival* (Viking 1987)

For a Conservative Prime Minister to call for a classless Britain is like M. Boulestin calling for a fat-free dinner.

Roy Jenkins commenting on the famous speech by Prime Minister John Major

Aristocracy was, of course, always an aspiration, not a reality. Few aristocrats were actually noble; many, if not most, were base. But calling them noble expressed a hope. Now we prefer to call everyone common, which also expresses a hope: that society can do without nobility – not individual examples of nobility lurking shamefacedly in private nooks and crannies and hidden away from the television cameras, but visible and public embodiments of nobility. For nobility, if it is to be acceptable nowadays, has to be disguised – in language, dress, and manners – so that its superiority doesn't stand out, lest that draw attention to the inferiority of everyone else. So when I say that aristocracy is missed, I do not mean – and I can't say this too often – that dukes and earls are missed; rather that the aristocratic idea, of which they used to be an embodiment, is what is missed. It is missed in art, architecture, literature, the media, the professions, the judiciary – though not in the armed forces where its continued presence never ceases to amaze and delight; and it is missed, most of all, in politics. This is not surprising since it was from the exigencies of politics that the felt need for the existence of a distinct and superior social class – a ruling class – originally sprang. For only by having such a class could a nation ensure for itself that necessary minority of citizens committed heart and soul to putting the public interest before the private interest, than which nothing is more essential for the good of all. In the nature of things the self-abnegation of this degree of nobility was too much to ask of ordinary mortals who had to earn their own living, but it was not too much to ask of that special social class whose privileges were designed to make them free to rise above common cares. Of course this ideal of public service was more honoured in the breach than in the observance. Only a minority of hereditary aristocrats lived up to it. Nevertheless, by maintaining this outward and visible form of aristocracy – the hereditary House of Lords, hereditary titles and the class system in general – the ideal itself, and the hope for its realization, was kept alive. True, even now, vestiges of the outward and invisible manifestations still live on. But little or nothing of the noble spirit. And it is the noble spirit that is missed. The nobles themselves are not missed, but nobility – the ideal of self-sacrificial public spirit – that *is* missed. Can we have the one without the other? Can we have political quality without social inequality? Can we abolish class distinctions and continue to have enough people willing to dedicate themselves to the public service?

Possibly; but it has to be said that the omens at present are not good. For the more socially equal British society becomes – and I will argue later that in many significant respects it is now more socially egalitarian than the United States – the less well our governing institutions seem to be working; so much less well that fewer and fewer citizens have any respect for them, to the point where the turnout at both local and general elections is unprecedentedly low. And never have MPs been held in lower esteem; not to mention other elite leaders, like doctors, lawyers, civil servants, bishops, and even, or especially, editors. How could it be otherwise, given the fact that, until not so long ago, the authority wielded by such dignitaries sprang quite as much from their position in the social hierarchy as from the height of their position on any particular professional or occupational ladder. This was even true of elected Members of Parliament. In theory, their authority sprang from having been elected – from the democratic principle; but in practice their social background – that is, the aristocratic principle – contributed quite as much. Of course the aristocratic principle was never the sole source of political authority; but until the symbolic abolition of the hereditary principle in the House of Lords, neither was the democratic principle. Indeed on its own, at least at present, that principle is proving insufficient. Today's classless MPs don't seem to cut the mustard, in spite of being elected. If they are from what used to be called gentlemanly stock, they are resented for being too grand; if they are not from that stock, they are found wanting for being too common. Possibly this is a transitional period. But Tocqueville warned that the most dangerous moment in the transition from aristocracy to democracy is during the final stage in the handover of power; when the aristocratic imprint is no longer visible enough in all the governing institutions to impress the democracy but just visible enough to promote its resentment; the moment when the ruling classes, traditionally taught to lead, are unlearning that lesson and ostentatiously disassociating themselves from that tradition, and the subordinate classes, traditionally taught to follow, are disassociating themselves obstreperously from their tradition. So where there used to be authority, there is now weakness and guilt, and where there used to be loyal subordination there is now bloody-mindedness and bitterness. In other words, neither of the public service traditions – leadership as much as followship – are any longer fully functioning. Just as the upper classes no longer feel an obligation to spend their lives in some form of public service – MPs, JPs, Whitehall mandarins, etc. – so the lower classes no longer feel a comparable obligation to lead their lives as dutiful workers, policemen, rankers, etc. Unfortunately, a democratic government, like every other form of government, needs authoritative people to run it and cannot function well without them, any more than it can function well without a deferential people. Possibly, in time, a new classless society will find a way of producing such people or find a way of functioning well without such people; but not in the current climate of anti-elitism, which, by poisoning the traditional well of aristocratic authority and prohibiting the search for a new elitist well to take its place, is only compounding the problem.

Nor does our current problem spring only from the decline in authority at the top. That is only half the problem. For the dissolving of the class system – a slow process, which could now be approaching the point of no return – has not only gravely diminished the authority of the old governing class but also, and just as important, the deference of the old governed class, both of which were equally essential ingredients in the success of Britain's tolerant, easy-going parliamentary democracy – the voluntary subordination of the latter being the complement of the former and vice versa. In short, our political institutions and their traditions nowadays lack two of their essential constitutional elements: the habit of authority in the few and the habit of voluntary subordination in the many. Current anti-elitism won't help to alleviate the second of these deficiencies any more than the first.

Why is there so little public recognition of the worrying significance of these developments? Part of the answer must be that Britain's social revolution, unlike France's and Russia's dramatic and violent ones, has been proceeding so gradually and peacefully, and over such a long period, that nobody has noticed that it has recently reached as far as it can go without fundamentally changing its character: by which I mean that the gentlemanly tradition has been adulterated to the point where it has become something almost entirely different – a plebeian tradition, which is not at all what Old Labour had in mind.

Old Labour's assumption was that slowly but surely every citizen would have an opportunity to become a member of the ruling class; that the political and social system would go on unchanged, except that instead of the necessary quota of authority figures prepared to dedicate their lives to the public weal coming from a relatively small section of the population, they would come henceforth from all sections of the people. In this way the class system would not fundamentally change, only become fairer. Throughout the nineteenth and twentieth centuries this evolution was taking place. First, the best and the brightest of the middle classes joined the ranks of the ruling class and then, in the course of the twentieth century, the best and brightest of the working class did likewise. The process was called upward social mobility – a process that could be likened to regular transfusions of new blood into the veins of the body politic; new blood that had the effect, much to the distress of the extreme radical point of view, of constantly giving the old body politic regular new leases of life. But none of this amounted to a fundamental social revolution since the new blood, having blended with the old blood, became itself bluish. Increasingly, working-class MPs, like Roy Jenkins, became honorific gentlemen – not only in name but also in accent, clothing, education, and social culture. Nor was this blending of new blood with blue blood limited only to Westminster and Whitehall; it happened, as we have seen, to the same degree in all fields – the legal profession, the Army, the Church of England, and so on. The new men, quite voluntarily, were only too pleased to fit into the gentlemanly mould. So although social egalitarianism proceeded at a pace, enough of the two essentials, authority at the top and deference at the bottom, survived to allow the civil spirit of British parliamentary democracy to continue to work. It was social egalitarianism adapted to the special nature of English history; social egalitarianism that envisaged broadening the aristocracy rather than destroying it. Slowly but surely, it enabled everyone with the necessary qualities to become a gentleman; to acquire the education of a gentleman, the manners of a gentleman, the employment that befits a gentleman, the respect that a gentleman commands, and, above all, the guaranteed economic security that is the material basis for the practice of these civilized, gentlemanly virtues.

When Old Labour reformers criticized Britain as a society of first- and second-class citizens, they meant the old divide between gentlemen and players. In their New Jerusalem, however, everyone would be a first-class citizen; in other words, a gentleman. That is what they meant by a classless society: a nation of gentlemen; a nation of active, public-spirited, freedom-loving citizens all endowed with gentlemanly virtues. Undoubtedly this served as a conservative force, placing limits on political and social equality, since even Old Labour was reluctant to let the gentlemanly baby out with the aristocratic bath water. In theory it was in favour of complete equality, but not to the point of destroying the very things about England – in a word, its civility – that it thought the nation, as its birthright, ought to have more of. England's ruling class, Old Labour was prepared to concede, was an exception, incomparably more worth preserving than German Junkers, Russian boyars, Chinese mandarins, or French caste-bound nobility, or even – as I shall try to be arguing later – the Anglo-Saxon WASP puritan ascendancy in the United States. For while it was easy enough for social reformers elsewhere to imagine getting rid of their unattractive and unpopular ruling classes, this was much more difficult in the case of England's gentlemanly class, if only because of the enormous gap its elimination would make to every aspect of the nation's life from politics to sport. No question, in England's case, of just cutting out rotten wood; more like taking an axe to the whole tree.

Another truth was also beginning to dawn on the political class in general: that a classless democracy that required every citizen to be active in politics on an informed and rational basis could not possibly produce stable democratic government; indeed would be bound instead to lead to a mass of conflicting views that would become all the more difficult to reconcile as the intellectual confidence of the group and individuals holding them increased, which would be bound to happen eventually as a result of universal education. So far from a more educated, sophisticated electorate making participatory democracy easier – as J. S. Mill assumed – it would in practice make it to all intents and purposes impossible. From which it followed that the only hope for a stable and effective democracy was a combination of active political participation by a few and passive trust by the many – the very combination, as it happened, into which by happy accident of history and of national genius the English aristocratic tradition had managed to evolve. For example, in his book *Britain Against Itself*, published in 1982, the American political guru Samuel Beer, much admired by Old Labour, saw the political culture of Britain as 'a balance or integration of two orientations, the modern and the traditional . . . values of hierarchy and organic connection that were medieval in origin adapted to and strengthened by successive systems of stratification, even as power and participation were extended. As deference, these hierarchical attitudes supported much independent authority for government, respect for leadership in political and organizational life, and in the bureaucracy a due sense of subordination and super ordination.' Moreover, he notes approvingly, as these attitudes descending from the traditional order qualified the liberating spirit of modern democracy, so also an attachment to custom, precedent, and history moderated the scientific thrust of modern rationalism.' So reverence for the old order and the ceremonies of the past, he concluded, made sense, and something immensely valuable to Britain as a whole might be lost if they were abandoned.

And so aristocracy, until recently, was recognized by serious reformers, at the very least, as something precious that had been lost. It is that recognition of loss that has changed, to be replaced, sad to say, by dismissive expressions of good riddance. Whereas the old consensus, backed by Old Labour and the Old Tories, had to do with a shared respect for gentlemanly values and for the institutions that had been shaped by those values, the new consensus, also backed by the New Conservatives and the New Labourites has to do with a shared contempt for the same values and the same institutions.

A hundred years ago Alfred Marshall, the great liberal – in the old sense – economist wrote: 'the question is not whether all men will ultimately be equal – that they will certainly not – but whether progress will not go on steadily, if slowly, till . . . every man is a gentleman'. A Utopian ideal? Very probably, but one wholly compatible with the spirit of our constitution. Today's radicals in all parties, however, see progress very differently, leading in fact to the point when no man is a gentleman – a dystopian ideal that is in danger of being realised with truly terrifying rapidity.

With the benefit of hindsight one can see that this change was bound to come given the dramatic explosion of radical populism, social egalitarianism, and 'me-first-ism' that occurred all over the world in the 1960s. For as a consequence of her unique success in banking down the fires of social revolution in the eighteenth and nineteenth centuries – avoiding anything comparable to the Jacksonian revolution in the United States – Britain still had so many more historic roots than any other country – previously a source of pride – for radicals to want to pull up. In fact traces of the dreaded aristocracy could still be found among all the elites, legal, military, ecclesiastic, and even technocratic, rendering almost every British national institution vulnerable to the charge of having committed, and still committing, crimes against the people. Hence Mr Blair's difficulties in finding a satisfactory replacement for the hereditary elements in the House of Lords, a meritocratic senate being scarcely less offensive to today's anti-elitists than an aristocratic one. So it was not so much that the forces unleashed in the 1960s were stronger in Britain than anywhere else as that the values and ideals those forces most abhorred – gentlemanliness in particular and social hierarchy in general – while peripheral in America and on the Continent were still central in Britain. So while all over the free world civic and political cultures were altered in the 1960s, only in Britain was the resulting fragmentation so great as to leave all classes, from the proverbial duke to the proverbial dustman, uncertain as to who they were and where they stood.

Matters were made only worse by the arrival in the 1980s of Mrs Thatcher – a force as destructive of gentlemanliness as any in the 1960s, not because she was against gentlemanliness in principle but because she blamed the gentlemanly tradition of *noblesse oblige* paternalism for the Conservative Party's post-war flirtation with neo-corporatist economic policies. In her eyes, aristocratic paternalism had resulted in tolerating a conspiracy between big business and the large trade unions to do down the self-employed, skilled workers, and small businessmen – the petite bourgeoisie. Moreover, she had come to the conclusion that her aim of purging the body politic of the socialist or collectivist virus justified a more ruthless use of State power than was allowed by the old gentlemanly tradition, which she dismissed as 'wet'. To this end she was prepared to risk, indeed to court, civil strife, as became clear when she bravely and successfully confronted Arthur Scargill's miners' strike, which in fact amounted to a mini-insurrection. Unlike Baldwin with the General Strike, her rhetoric was anything but conciliatory, remaining as ferocious after victory as before it. Hers was the use of English State power familiar to the Irish down the ages, but not used so brazenly on the mainland itself since the panic following the Napoleonic Wars. Very probably she had no alternative. Certainly no other British Prime Minister, Conservative or Labour, during the last three-quarters of the twentieth century would have thought her almost Cromwellian rhetoric proper. And it is indicative of the coarseness in the New Conservative ranks that they should have mistaken those earlier aristocratic scruples for nothing more than 'a lack of guts'.

In any case the confrontation, undertaken in defiance of the traditional aristocratic aversion to confrontation, succeeded, constituting the first example of pure petit-bourgeois triumphalism in English history. Having on its own broken the back of the trade union movement, the anti-aristocratic petit bourgeois elements of the Conservative Party at long last felt confident enough to govern untraditionally, not only without the tutelage of the aristocratic tradition but explicitly in defiance of that tradition. Not long after came the formal admission under New Labour of socialism's defeat in the class war and the lifting of the socialist threat to expropriate private property, fear of which throughout the late nineteenth and twentieth centuries had been the reason for England's aristocracy and haute bourgeoisie to make common cause in the first place. But with victory in the class war assured, they no longer needed each other. Under the new circumstances, not only was aristocratic tutelage judged by the bourgeoisie to be no longer an asset but rather to have become a positive liability. For if New Labour was now a pro-capitalist party, and therefore unable to continue beating the economic equality drum, interested only in equalizing social status (abolishing the monarchy, the House of Lords, hereditary privilege, Oxford elitism, fox-hunting, etc.) and no longer committed to equalizing wealth, what was wrong with that? Indeed, from a free-market point of view, and in particular from the trans-atlantic point of view of the great conservative media moguls, might there not be quite a lot right with that? New Labour's removal of the threat to property had thus altered the balance of power in British politics, allowing the bourgeois bulk of the Conservative Party, which only accepted the aristocratic tradition as a marriage of convenience, to show what, out of prudence, they had previously kept hidden: their anti-gentlemanly social chip on the shoulder. As a result, we now have a modernizing, classless political consensus consisting of a non-socialist New Labour Party and a pro-capitalist New Conservative Party, neither of which is much concerned to conserve the historic institutions. Instead of two socially conservative parties, we now have two iconoclastic, and in that metaphorical sense radical, parties. As a force for change, capitalism in Britain was always likely to be a more socially dissolvent force than socialism. Indeed socialism, by frightening and therefore slowing down the capitalist horses, acted more as a brake than an accelerator, a brake that has now, for better or worse, been lifted.

So from both parties now come the same tune, the rich are all right so long as they do not give themselves superior airs (that is, behave like gentlemen), and do not adhere to any standards that are superior to those currently recommended by the popular press. Nowadays, to a greater extent in England than anywhere else in the world, certainly greater than in the United States, classiness has become a badge of shame and guilt; nobody, least of all a politician, if he can possibly help it, wants to admit membership of a superior class and wherever possible will do his or her best to behave and speak in such a manner as to suggest membership of an inferior class – not, heaven forbid, a poorer class, but a less cultivated and civilized class.* *Écrasez l'infâme*, cry our contemporary Voltaires, as much in the *Guardian* as in the *Sun*, who can't rest until the last Oxbridge elitist don is strangled by the guts of the last Covent Garden Opera House aesthete.

---

* Consider Douglas Hurd's pathetic attempt – during his bid to succeed Mrs Thatcher – to prove himself the son of an impoverished tenant farmer. The story is told, with some embarrassment, in Hurd's memoirs.

What has happened to the BBC, which was twentieth-century Britain's most admired creation, is a lamentable example of this officially inspired de-classing process. Having hitherto seen its role as being to raise the nation's cultural sights, it is now required to dedicate its expertise to the task of persuading its viewers – not so much its listeners – to drop their aitches. Foreign observers cannot understand what is happening. How, they ask, can Britain, which used to be the most civil of societies, have become, in so short a time, the most uncivil? True, there are deep-seated and cumulative impersonal forces at work arising from changes in occupation, property distribution, education and mobility, but these are not peculiar to Britain. What is peculiar to Britain is a set of political circumstances that has allowed New Labour to save its face over its renunciation of socialism and adoption of capitalism by seizing with irresponsible zeal on the goal of social equality, which in turn has forced the Conservative Party, in an effort to keep capitalism on side, to dump the gentleman in favour of Essex Man – to the point where, if things are allowed to go on as at present, the Anglo-Saxon patrician tradition will be safer in the United States than in Great Britain.

Gaetano Mosca, in his great classic, *The Ruling Class*, warned a hundred years ago that something like this might happen. 'At a certain stage of democratic development', he wrote, 'a clique will detach itself from the middle classes and, in the rush to win the better posts, try to seek leverage in the instincts and appetites of the more populous classes, telling them that political equality will mean almost nothing unless it goes hand in hand with economic equality.' As we know, that socialist moment came all too soon, and, thank heaven, has passed – without doing much damage. Now, however, another middle-class clique, also in the rush to win the better posts, is seeking leverage in the instincts and appetites of the populous classes, telling them that political equality means almost nothing unless it goes hand in hand with social equality: a twenty-first-century variation on egalitarianism – this one backed by capitalism – even less likely than socialism to produce a better, still less a remoralized, social and political order.

Four

The tableau which American society presents is, if I can put it this way, covered with a democratic coat, but beneath it from time to time the old colours of aristocracy break through.

I am firmly convinced that an aristocracy cannot be founded anew in the world; but I think that by associating ordinary citizens can constitute very rich bodies, very influential and very strong, in other words, an aristocratic being. In this way one could gain many of the greatest political advantages of aristocracy without its injustices or dangers.

Alexis de Tocqueville

The absence of barriers in America's political democracy . . . has not prevented the gradual growth of an estate of 'aristocrats' alongside the crude plutocracy of property . . . and the slow, but generally overlooked growth of this 'aristocracy' is just as important for the history of American culture.

Max Weber

The Bush dynasty differs from other American families that have mixed wealth with political prominence. While the Kennedys and the Rockefellers may have a sense of entitlement, they also display a sense of *noblesse oblige* – what one might call an urge to repay, with charitable contributions and public service, their good fortunes. The Bushs don't have that problem; there are no philanthropists or reformers in the clan. They seek public office but, if anything, they seem to feel that the public is there to serve them.

> Attributed to Paul R. Krugman reviewing *American Dynasty: Aristocracy, Fortune, and the Politics of Deceit in the House of Bush* by Kevin Phillips in *New York Review of Books*, February 26, 2004

In its early years the United States of America was a classless society, and still cherishes that golden memory rather as European nostalgics – with less justification – still cherish a golden memory of feudalism in the Middle Ages. But it is important to emphasize that America was classless, not because of having got rid of classes but because of not having had them in the first place. True, early on, some of the independent states – and not only in the South – were on the verge of creating titles of nobility, but the War of Independence intervened to nip these aspirations in the bud, thereby ensuring that the citizens of the new Republic, in the event, were indeed conceived and born, in a manner of speaking, equal; by which I mean that theirs was a uniquely high quality of equality, a uniquely classy order of class-lessness.

Not that it could have been otherwise, given the seventeenth-century provenance of the early Puritan and Calvinist settlers who adhered to the most morally select of all creeds, believing themselves to be equal in the same way as the biblical Israelites believed themselves to be equal: all equally chosen, that is, by God. But by no stretch of the imagination could such people be described as common. More plausibly they would have to be described as divine-right aristocrats who, being already lords of Christ, felt no need to become mere English lords; felt no desire to dress up in ermine or to live in palaces, or to put a crown upon their heads, or to have blue blood or noble quarterings, since they already had within them a spiritual superiority that transcended all such worldly baubles. True, there were no Puritan rulers or ruled; no domineering bishops or subservient laymen, and in that sense there was no hierarchy, except that most formidable hierarchy of all: between saints and sinners, between the saved and the damned.

It was not only a question of moral superiority since, intellectually and educationally, they were also in a class of their own. Professor Sheldon Wolin, in his excellent *Tocqueville Between Two Worlds: The Making of a Political and Theoretical Life* – to which I am deeply indebted throughout this chapter – quotes the great French political philosopher as saying of the early Puritan settlers, 'that they brought with them the most advanced "democratic and Republican theories", an "austerity of manners", "wonderful elements of order and morality"; a strict legal code, and all of "the general principles upon which modern constitutions rest": citizen participation, especially in the voting of taxes, the accountability of officials, individual freedom, and trial by jury'. And another French commentator on early America was equally amazed at their standard of intelligence. According to Michel Chevalier, the mind of a French peasant was full of 'biblical parables' and 'gross superstitions', whereas the American farmer had been 'initiated' into 'the conquest of the human mind' that began with the Reformation. 'The great scriptural traditions are harmoniously combined in his mind with the principles of modern science as taught by Bacon and Descartes, with the doctrine of moral and religious independence proclaimed by Luther, and with the still more recent notions of political freedom.' The common people in America, unlike those of Europe, therefore, were fit to take part in public affairs. They did not need to be governed since they were able to govern themselves.

In early America every citizen also had relatively easy access to the ownership of land – which in Europe at that time was the essential qualification for gentlemanly status. So America from the very beginning was a property-owning democracy in which all citizens lived on their own land and were independent in their circumstances. Consequently, there were no peasants or proletarians. Under such con-ditions – conditions widely regarded as typical as late as the Civil War – it only made sense to speak of a labouring class and a leisured class if all citizens were included in *both*. True, strictly speaking, there were no gentlemen, but that was only because there were no commoners either. So in early America not only was every citizen his own priest – master of his soul – and his own sage – master of his mind – but also master of his own estate.

Most important of all, of course, there was the brute fact of black slavery, which meant that even the humblest and poorest white was born immensely superior by reason of belonging to a master race. What he had in common with the grandest and richest of his fellow freemen was incomparably greater than what he had in common with any black slave. A similar white sense of racial superiority existed in the Old World as well, but not to anything like the same extent. There, it was at least partially mitigated by considerations of class: that is to say, a white English labourer would not by any means necessarily regard himself as the superior of a black king or chief. Indeed when the pre-Enlightenment English explorers first encountered the native North Americans in the seventeenth century they unquestioningly credited them with operating the same kind of civilized hierarchical social system as their own. They therefore accorded royal status to black and brown leaders, aristocratic status to the sub-chiefs, and so on and so forth down the social scale.

By the time United States was born, however, such old-fashioned ideas, which ignored all the new, supposedly scientific, discoveries about all blacks and browns being inferior to all whites, seemed as out of date as believing that the earth was flat. To Enlightenment Man it was a self-evident truth that black and brown savages were not the equal of whites; indeed it was a self-evident fact that, by all the Enlightenment criteria – education, culture, literacy, etc. – they were immeasurably inferior. This, at the time, was not a reactionary view. Quite the opposite: it was at the cutting edge of scientific thought. Except to a crazy romantic like Rousseau, it was clearly the sheerest nonsense to treat a naked jibbering Caliban as if he was noble. In any case the American, true to his Enlightenment principles, no longer believed in kings, princes, and aristocrats. So, far from the existence of a social hierarchy among 'the brutes' – as even Edmund Burke called them – being seen as a mark of their civilization, it was taken as further and conclusive proof of their incorrigible backwardness. Not so, however, in Britain, where it was seen as their redeeming feature – at least when doing so served the purposes of Britain's governance, as it very often did. To illustrate Britain's mixture of pre-Enlightenment and post-Enlightenment attitudes, David Cannadine, in his invaluable *Ornamentalism: How the British Saw their Empire*, tells the following story:

> In the summer of 1881 King Kalakaua of Hawaii was visiting England and, in the course of an extensive round of social engagements, he found himself the guest at a party given by Lady Spencer. Also attending were the Prince of Wales, who would eventually become King Edward VII, and the German Crown Prince, who was his brother-in-law and the future Kaiser. The Prince of Wales insisted that the [Hawaiian] King should take precedence over the Crown Prince, and when his brother-in-law objected, he offered the following pithy and trenchant justification: 'Either the brute is a King, or he's a common or garden nigger; and if the latter what's he doing here?'

Such ambivalence continued to the very end of the Empire. I remember Harold Macmillan during his valedictory tour of Africa in 1961 – no previous serving prime minister had ever visited these south-Saharan colonies and his visit was only to wave them goodbye – telling the accompanying reporters, of whom I was one, how much more at home he felt staying in the Palace of the Sarduana of Sokoto, the black hereditary ruler of Northern Nigeria (whom he affectionately compared to a Scottish Highland chieftain) than he expected to feel when staying – his next port of call – with the white Prime Minister of the Central African Federation, Roy Welensky, a former engine driver and boxing champion. So far as Britain was concerned, class consciousness always counted for as much as, if not more than, race consciousness. There again the English penchant for snobbery served a benign purpose. For while enslaving non-royal Africans might or might not be morally repugnant, enslaving African kings quite definitely smacked of *lèse-majesté*. So, whereas the Old World principle of attaching a different status to individuals allowed at least some blacks and browns to escape humiliation on the basis of colour or race, the New World's refusal to recognize any of the old feudal distinctions made sure that all blacks and browns were consigned equally to the dung heap, and all the white Americans given pride of place as members of an hereditary master race.

Right from the start, therefore, American citizens were the proudest of the proud, all equally superior to everybody else in terms of their Protestant religion, their Enlightenment scientific and political principles, and, above all, by the colour of their skin. Given so many fundamental superiorities in common it is scarcely surprising that such comparatively superficial material differences – that some lived in larger houses than others and owned more acres – paled into insignificance. In the things that really mattered they were equal, and the moral, religious, and intellectual bonds binding them together were infinitely more important than the wealth barriers dividing them.

So while, strictly speaking, a classless society, early America was not a society with which today's anti-elitists would wish to identify themselves. For quite as much of the aristocratic principle – rule by the best – went into its formation as of the democratic principle, rule by the people.

This, I believe, was the aspect of early American democracy that impressed Tocqueville most: not, as is usually supposed, the absence of aristocracy but rather its unexpected presence, in particular the existence there from the outset of citizens willing and able to act and think disinterestedly and heroically about the destiny and freedom of the nation – the very role the French nobility had played in the Middle Ages before Louis XIV in the seventeenth century had reduced them to a coterie of courtiers. Indeed Tocqueville credited the Pilgrim Fathers with suffusing the early American Republic with a spirit of aristocracy from the very beginning: not aristocracy understood as a distinct political class empowered by the constitution to govern, but rather as a social, cultural, and religious force whose *mœurs* (his word) would always give American civil society the confidence to resist the centralized power of the State – something in the Old World only done successfully by an aristocracy – and ensure the active civic participation of the whole nation, with every citizen obliged, as aristocrats in the Old World had ideally been, to put the nation's destiny before their own.

Before going to America, Tocqueville had simply taken it for granted that conditions of social equality could not possibly produce citizens of such exceptionally high political quality; such high-minded persons dedicated to the protection of the constitutional order itself, he assumed, could only be grown in a higher quality of social soil, one enriched by generations of power and privilege. The occasional 'natural aristocrat' might be found, rather as the occasional rare bloom is found growing wild in a country hedgerow; but inevitably such sports of nature would be few and far between. So for the numbers to begin to constitute a civil association powerful and bonded enough to energize and inspire a great nation only a hereditary nobility would suffice.

As a result of his visit to America, however, Tocqueville modified this view. For his experiences in early nineteenth-century America revealed to him a degree of civil virtue in townships across the land that convinced him that, given the favourable circumstances of the New World, ordinary citizens without any hereditary privileges could also practise these altruistic political virtues, not quite at the level of an inherited aristocracy perhaps, but at a level that would pass muster. The opportunities of the New World, he believed, had transformed bourgeois and plebeian geese into aristocratic swans, capable of amazing flights, not only of economic initiative but also of political innovation. Equally impressive and surprising, he noted, was the sophisticated citizenship displayed by non-political citizens who conscientiously and trustingly supported such initiatives and innovations. True, there were no peasants or proletarians in early nineteenth-century America where, as we have seen, access to the ownership of land – the mark of a gentleman in Europe – was relatively easy for all. But even so, except briefly in the southern states, there were no hereditary aristocrats either. No wonder, therefore, sailing down the Mississippi one day, he was happy to conclude that: 'there is one thing that America proves conclusively and that which I have previously doubted: it is that the middle classes can govern a state'; by which he meant that in America the middle class would shoulder the aristocratic burden and themselves become witness to everything the New World so sadly lacked, which included high statesmanship, high culture, good taste and manners, grace and loyalty. To me that sounds rather like wishful thinking that inside the fat body of American democracy there was at least a thin spirit of aristocracy trying to get out; more than that, succeeding in getting out – particularly in the patrician-run 'city states' of Boston, Philadelphia, Charleston, and New York.

On his second visit to America, however, Tocqueville was much less impressed, if only because by then the onrush of industrialization was already beginning to put an end to Jefferson's agrarian Utopia; already beginning to introduce enormous differentials of wealth between master and man, employer and employee, hirer and hired, the property owner and the property-less. The economic opportunities of the

new continent were also proving even more tempting than
he had supposed; so much more that such dreams as the
middle class were dreaming had become more material than
political, more selfish than altruistic, with the best and
brightest more concerned to make money as employers
exploiting their workers than to earn fame and glory as
politicians directing the nation's destiny. As a result, by the
time Andrew Jackson came to presidential power in the
1830s, the new nation's capital was beginning to resemble
Babylon rather than Athens. But although these material-
istic manifestations dented Tocqueville's faith in the new
democracy, he stuck optimistically to his central insight:
that because the New World had never suffered under a
quasi-feudal aristocracy, it had never had cause, as revolutionary France had had, to ferment so fierce a degree of
anti-aristocratic rage as to dissolve respect for all forms of
superiority – spiritual, moral, and material. So, as Professor
Wolin puts it, 'in a climate un-poisoned alike by irresponsible privilege and revolutionary rage, the American high
achievers – clergy, rich merchants, lawyers, intelligentsia –
could legitimately without guilt act as a galvanizing force
and the low achievers – i.e. demos – without shame act as
a moderating force.'

Such optimism about American democracy that survived
Tocqueville's second visit thus rested on the assumption
that it was less likely than European democracy to want
to drag everything down. For whereas in the Old World
everything elevating and superior – from good manners to
religion – had become suspect because of association with

a discredited feudal system, in America all these splendid things could start again with a clean slate; without, so to speak, 'previous form'. What did this mean in practice? It meant, for example, that unlike the aspiring European bourgeoisies who had found all the prestigious jobs in Church and State already monopolized by tenaciously ensconced noblemen, their American counterparts were lucky enough to find instead a vacuum at the top just waiting to be filled. No other national bourgeoisie had ever had such an easy run for their money or found so few obstacles – either of reactionary ideology or traditional privilege – blocking their way. Instead of being made to feel nouveau-riche parvenus or illegitimate upstarts, the American bourgeoisie, right from the start, could and did regard themselves as the genuine article, with no cause to develop chips on their shoulders.

By the same token, the absence of a feudal experience also worked wonders for the American working class, which, being unburdened by memories of institutional serfdom, was that much more easily persuadable that capitalist bottom-dogdom was the lowest rung of an ascending ladder and not, as their European counterparts had reason to fear, a preordained and inescapable fate. The absence of a feudal past not only enabled America's bourgeoisie to feel more comfortable in their skins than their European counterparts, but enabled her working class to do so too. America's industrialization, therefore, got off to a unique start: an owning bourgeois class without neo-feudal guilt about superiority, and a proletarian working class without shameful hang-ups about inferiority. For inequality, therefore, it was a miraculous turn-up for the book, providing at any rate its capitalist manifestation with a new world to conquer.

Tocqueville, an aristocrat himself, relished this New World lack of guilt about inequality, in such marked contrast to the French Revolution's Jacobinical extremism, seeing in it a marvellous opportunity for the New World to replace an illegitimate form of inequality, sustained only by repressing the human spirit, with a modern republican spirit of inequality designed to liberate it. In the New World top democrats – appropriately republicanized into senators – had become once again acceptable, in the same way that kings had become suitably republicanized into presidents.

So without consciously willing it – indeed in spite of consciously willing the opposite – American democracy had released inequality from the burden of its feudal past. But so, to a lesser extent, had English aristocracy, the praises of which Tocqueville never ceased to sing. For it too – compared to its *ancien régime* counterparts on the Continent – had also gone a long way towards sharing power with the bourgeoisie; towards allowing the middle class to demonstrate its capacity to govern. These reassuringly non-populist – even anti-populist – democratizing processes, which Tocqueville describes in his great work *Democracy in America*, therefore, were happening almost as much in Old England as in New England; were indeed Anglo-Saxon processes, the American Revolution of 1776 having been as much about establishing aristocratic democracy in the United States as the English revolution of 1688 had been about doing the same for aristocratic democracy in England.

And not only *establishing* aristocratic democracy, since from the perspective of the twenty-first century America's written constitution may prove to have been an even longer lasting bastion against majority tyranny and mass radicalism than England's unwritten constitution and hereditary House of Lords. Indeed Tocqueville never allows his readers to over-look these shared affinities: he always refers to the Americans as Anglo-Americans, and leaves his readers in little doubt that the greatness of America owed quite as much to its Englishness – the principal characteristic of which, in his view, was enlightened aristocracy – as to its democracy. Had he lived longer into the nineteenth century – long enough to notice how half a century of unrestricted immigration produced a mass of second-class non-Anglo-Saxon Ameri-can citizens – he would not have failed to notice that the resemblance between the two democracies was growing ever closer. For by then both democracies were being increas-ingly run by patrician minorities; this at a period, moreover, when both ruling minorities were beginning to see them-selves as leaders of a master race destined to secure law and order across the entire surface of the globe.

By the middle of the nineteenth century Jefferson's agri-cultural ideal of a nation entirely made up of citizens of equal social status – all property owners on the same edu-cational and cultural level, if not all equally rich – had been superseded by a nation with a much more clearly stratified social system: not a de jure social system based on a theory of inherited ranks, as in Europe, but a de facto or practical social system based on race, religion, and the date of arrival in the United States. Under this system, white Anglo-Saxon Protestants descended from the Puritans just happened to be at the top – because they were America's senior citizens – and the blacks, just because they were considered to be intellectually inferior, were at the bottom. Interposed between them was an ever-increasing number of non-Anglo-Saxon religious and ethnic layers whose members did the menial work, had no influence on society, were not self-conscious, and produced no national – as against urban – leaders of their own. It was, and to some extent still is, a bafflingly complex system of overlapping social distinctions, the subtleties of which are as difficult to grasp for the British as ever the British class system has been to the Americans. Was an Irish–American more American, for example, than a Spanish–American, or a German–American more American than a Polish–American, or a Jewish–American more American than a Japanese American? The answer seems to have altered with the times, but not for the black Americans who remained at the rock bottom, or for the Wasps who remained at the top. And at the very pinnacle sat 'the Wasp ascendancy', recognizable as a group because its members – mostly from New England – had either known each other from birth or were blood relations – the 'cousinage', as it was called. Moreover, they spoke with the same accents, went to the same tailors, holidayed at the same resorts – not to mention having been at the same schools and universities – and were also richer on average and enjoyed substantially more leverage than many Americans. For these reasons they had supplied the role models followed by other

Americans, whether Wasp or non-Wasp, who were on the way up in the world.*

Only against this background can the much-rehearsed story of Abraham Lincoln's rise from log cabin to White House be put into proper perspective; not, as it is usually presented, as a classic illustration of the extent of American egalitarianism so much as a classic demonstration of the hereditary privileges pertaining in America to the Anglo-Saxons. About the facts, there is no question. Lincoln was indeed born in a log cabin. His father was indeed a casual labourer and his mother both illiterate and illegitimate. But these, in the circumstances of the time, were not the crucial facts.† These were that both his parents were white Anglo-Saxon Protestants, his father's forbears having come over from England as early as 1637.

Nor had the Lincoln family always been poor and humble: the future president's maternal grandfather, at the time of the Declaration of Independence, had been a captain in the Virginia Militia who, on the advice of his close friend, Daniel Boone, had sought his fortune on the frontier where – like so many others – he was killed by Indians. Hence the family's decline into poverty. Even so, in American terms, the Lincoln blood was, so to speak, bluish and his lineage aristocratic. In

---

* See Joseph W. Alsop, *I've Seen the Best of It* (New York: Norton, 1992).
† For these facts, and much else in this chapter, I am deeply indebted to E. Digby Baltzell's *The Protestant Establishment: Aristocracy and Caste in America* (New York: Random House, 1964; London: Secker & Warburg, 1965).

British terms, his elevation to president was more like the son of an impoverished early Victorian gentleman becoming prime minister – an equally possible scenario in Britain in the mid-nineteenth century. So while the story certainly demonstrates the existence in antebellum America of equality of opportunity among the white Anglo-Saxon Protestants, that is not saying very much more than that in Victorian England there was an equality of opportunity among gentlemen.

Jan Morris, in her *Lincoln: A Foreigner's Quest*, compares him to the narrator in Evelyn Waugh's *Brideshead Revisted* – 'the clever, unimaginative, impressionable young man out of a lower social stratum bewitched by an upper class style, *and perhaps discerning it as properly his own*' (my italics). In effect, therefore Lincoln's ascent from log cabin to White House was not from the depths to the heights, as it is often presented, but rather from the top floor, so to speak, to the penthouse. Naturally enough, therefore, the President's son, Robert Todd Lincoln, bore none of the scars of a parvenu and took to the aristocratic life as to the manner born. In fact he soon became a member of all the most snobbish and exclusive Wasp clubs in Chicago, New York, and Washington DC, with an honoured place in the *Social Register*, America's *Almanach de Gotha*, something which, at that time and for nearly a century thereafter, few non-Wasps could expect to achieve.

Even by the twentieth century things were much the same. Incredibly enough, for example, the family of the great Henry and William James, usually regarded on the other side of the Atlantic as the very epitome of American Brahminism –

did not really qualify for that status. For as Louis Menand tells us:

> The Jameses were not Brahmins. They were not even New Englanders. They were descended on both sides from Irish immigrants, and although the Jameses now seem as American as the [Ralph Waldo] Emersons or the [Oliver Wendell] Holmeses, to people like the Emersons and the Holmeses they seemed rather distinctively Irish. To understand Henry or William James, Holmes once explained to his English friend Frederick Pollock, 'One must remember their Irish blood.' 'In their speech, singularly mature and picturesque, as well as vehement, the Gaelic (Irish) element in their descent always showed,' is the way Emerson's son Edward remembered the family. The Jameses enjoyed great social success, but they knew themselves to be, subtly but irreducibly, outsiders – even in their charming fashion, upstarts.

Nor had much changed by the 1930s. As rich a tycoon as Joseph P. Kennedy, father of Jack Kennedy, is on record then as saying: 'How long does a family have to live here before *he* stops being called an Irish–American?' True, money could get you very far up the scale, particularly in city politics, and even – thirty years on – into the White House; but getting into the White House was one thing: penetrating into the inner reaches of the law firms where the power of corporate America lay, even in President

Kennedy's day, was quite another. Of course Washington, DC, and the higher reaches of Wall Street were not America, and I do not want to exaggerate the degree of ethnic exclusion in the country as a whole. In all the great New England cities, like Boston and Philadelphia, the ethnic minorities had long had their own social ladders that met and intermingled with the Wasp social ladder at the top and had done so for several generations; furthermore, city politics, depending as they did on immigrant votes, had always been dominated by ethnic politicians, like Mayor La Guardia in New York or Mayor Curley in Boston. But when it came to the management of diplomatic and international affairs, or of the great Ivy League institutions of higher education, or of literature and culture generally, or, most important of all, national security, Wasp leadership was quite simply taken for granted. The senior ranks of the Office of Strategic Studies in the Second World War, and of the Central Intelligence Agency in the Cold War, were as automatically and unquestioningly filled by gentlemanly alumni from Harvard and Yale as the senior ranks of MI5 and MI6, in the same period, had been by gentlemanly graduates of Oxford and Cambridge.

So at the highest political levels the New England Wasp ruling families were scarcely less dominant than the old English ruling families. But not in theory, and therein lay the most significant difference. Whereas the English aristocracy at least half believed in the idea of a society stratified by inherited status – believed, that is, in its God-given right to rule – virtually all the Wasp aristocracy firmly believed, from the start, in majority rule, the equality of man, and equality of opportunity. They would not have considered for a moment having a constitution that legitimized any hereditary House of Lords, which they would have regarded as irrational, archaic, primitive, and even barbaric. Their right to rule, by contrast, *stood to reason*: because they had been in America from the creation, so to speak, Wasps were quite obviously the best people suited to do the job in the spirit of the Founding Fathers; the best people, that is, to preserve liberal democracy (particularly its laissez-faire dimensions); and if the waves of new Americans did not like America's version of liberal democracy – which included, among many other unpopular things, allowing free speech to communist atheists – it was their duty, as aspirant Americans, at least to pretend to. And the impoverished immigrants, most of whom did not even speak English, were quite happy to do so, being only too thankful for small mercies. New World egalitarianism came with a condition attached: every American was equal, but only if he or she was prepared *not* to be different; prepared, that is, to be as Waspish as the Wasps themselves, if not more so, in the same way that Catholic converts are often more Catholic than the Pope.

So unlike in Britain, where inequality was at least half-heartedly backed by a High Tory doctrine about the prescriptive superiority of blue blood, in America it was only an unintended consequence of the nation's impeccably liberal open-door immigration policy, which had produced wave after wave of docile, deferential, malleable, undemanding second-, third-, and fourth-class citizens who knew their place, not in theory but in fact. True, every new wave ratcheted the previous wave up a rung, but so long as the immigration gates were still open there was always another wave of vulnerable immigrants only too happy to fill the gap at the bottom. Nothing about this was in conflict with the precepts of liberal democracy: quite the contrary, since the Statue of Liberty welcoming the immigrants was the very symbol of that democracy. But such a way of combining the theory of liberal democracy with the practice of social inequality was, it has to be said, open only to God's own country. For only in that country was there an opportunity, open to every immigrant, to win his spurs as a hundred per cent, property-owning and independent-minded American by acquiring land out West. At least that was the myth to which lip service was paid long after it had ceased to accord with reality. In fact by the end of the nineteenth century the so-called Wild West had become more a fashionable finishing school or adventure playground for the sons of rich Wasps, like the future President Teddy Roosevelt, than a proving ground for poor immigrants.* Both the author Owen Wister, in his classic *The Virginian*, and Frederick Remington, in his equally famous picture *The Last Cavalier* – both created by patrician Wasps who mythologized the West – leave us in no doubt on that score. For example, Wister, in a famous article, wrote:

---

* See chapter seven of John Lukacs's *Philadelphia: Patricians and Philistines, 1900–1950* (New York: Farrar, Straus and Giroux, 1981).

To survive in the clean cattle country requires a spirit of adventure, courage and self-sufficiency: you will not find any Poles or Huns or Russian Jews [i.e. immigrants] in that district; it stands as yet untainted by the benevolence of Baron Hirsch [another immigrant]. Even in the cattle country the respectable Swedes settled chiefly to farming, and are seldom horsemen . . . The Frenchman today is seen at his best inside a house; he can paint and he can play comedy; but he seldom climbs a new mountain. The Italian has forgotten Columbus and sells fruit; among the Spaniards and the Portuguese, no Cortez or Magellan is found today. Even in Prussia the Teutonist, too often a tame slippered animal, with his pedantic mind swaddled in a dressing gown. But the Anglo-Saxon is still forever homesick for out of doors.

Later the anti-ethnic, immigration angle is emphasized even more clearly. 'The Frontier', wrote Wister,

gave the Anglo-Saxon race a last chance: the race that was once again subjected to battles and darkness, rain and shine, to fierceness and the generosity of the desert. Destiny tried her latest experiments upon the Saxon, and plucking it from the library, the haystack and the gutter, set him upon his horse; then it was that, face to face with the internal simplicity of death, his modern guise fell away and he showed again the medieval man.

So, 'medieval man' for Wister and *The Last Cavalier* for Remington: both very far cries from the egalitarian version of the West as the place where poor immigrants had the inalienable right, as American citizens, to hack out a private plot of land for themselves. Nevertheless, at least in theory – or rather at least in dreams – all Americans enjoyed the right to become a citizen in the full property-owning and freestanding Jeffersonian manner.

Not after 1890, however. That was the momentous, history-changing year when the Census Bureau removed that fig leaf by declaring the open frontier officially closed for settlement, thereby exposing the ugly reality of what lay behind: the growing gulf in America between great wealth and abject poverty and, even more at odds with Jefferson's ideal of a classless society, the unmistakable tendency of each to become hereditary. This was not the only blow to America's idea of itself. Shortly thereafter came an even more serious one: the clanging shut of the hitherto wide-open immigration gates. In a country like America, dedicated to the proposition that all men are born equal and entirely lacking any traditional prescriptive national doctrine of inequality, a system of social stratification, in order to survive, has to have a non-doctrinal, practical, de facto basis – exactly the basis unrestricted immigration supplied. Shutting off unrestricted immigration, however, was bound, in the long run, to dissolve that basis. For while it had made sense and seemed perfectly fair to a first-generation Irish trucker, say, or to a first-generation Polish tailor, to leave national politics to the Wasps, it was bound to make slightly less sense and to seem slightly less fair to their sons, and make positively no sense at all to their grandsons, whilst to their great grandsons it would seem nothing short of a crying scandal. With each succeeding decade, therefore, the number of hyphenated Americans, too frightened to take the promise of American equality at face value, dwindled, a process enormously accelerated in the twentieth century by astonishing economic expansion, which made it relatively safe and easy, by the end of the century, for even first-generation, non-English-speaking *illegal* immigrants – such as those swimming across the Rio Grande from Mexico – to demand full and immediate access to their place in the American sun, without even being obliged to learn the English language.

But I am jumping ahead too fast. For in spite of two of the main struts justifying the Wasp hegemony having collapsed, it was still very much a force to be reckoned with in the late 1930s, as I can remember all too vividly. My brother and I had been sent to spend the summer holidays in Maine with eastern-educated, mellowly wealthy Wasp Republican grandee friends of my stepfather, Montagu Norman. At all times of the night and day their conversation consisted of fiery diatribes against President Roosevelt, not because of his quasi-socialist New Deal ideas – comparable anti-socialist ideological abuse was also commonplace in England at that period – but because of his defiance of caste by appointing Jews and other non-Wasp beneficiaries of the Ivy League quota system to his Cabinet and to the Supreme Court, and even appointing one black to the Federal Bench.

Quite simply, FDR believed in turning up the gas under the melting pot and our hosts believed, equally absolutely, in turning the gas down, if not off altogether. It was a profound clash of principles. While to the one the glory of America lay in an ever-increasing mix of races and religions, to the other it lay in maintaining for ever the supremacy of the Anglo-Saxons. The latter's raw kind of atavistic caste arrogance was something my brother and I had never heard before: quite unlike the affectionate and even admiring jokes being made by the English upper classes at the time about the dropped aitches of horny-handed Labour Cabinet Ministers like Jimmy Thomas. One particularly vile piece of doggerel directed at FDR's wife, Eleanor, quite as much as at the President himself, has stuck in my mind.

> You kiss the Negros
> I will kiss the Jews,
> We'll stay in the White House
> As long as we choose.

These passionately anti-ethnic prejudices were not limited only to the realm of politics. They also manifested themselves quite as much in the day- to-day social life of the smart-set swimming club, where non-Wasps even with the most impeccably classy credentials were made to feel noticeably unwelcome. For example, my brother and I were politely admonished for inviting along a friend of our own age who was the son of a distinguished historian at a Catholic university in Philadelphia. To our innocent eyes he had seemed irreproachably eligible – well dressed, well heeled, well spoken, well mannered, etc., etc. And so indeed he was: unmistakably upper-middle class. But *Irish–American* upper-middle class, which was not at all the same thing as being Wasp upper-middle class. What is more, as transpired later, my brother and I, being Roman Catholic, had also caused some eyebrows to rise, although in our case the Englishness of our Catholicism had come in handy as a saving grace.

FDR, as we now know, got his way, as he was bound to do since by the 1930s more Americans were living in the cities – where the ethnic minorities predominated – than in the rural areas where the Wasp writ still ran. In any case so severe was the challenge of the Depression, and so ostrich-like the rock-ribbed Republican response, that nothing could stop his policy of recruiting all the available talent, ethnic as well as Wasp, to meet it. In respect of bringing in new blood the Depression had something of the same effect on America's system of caste stratification as the Second World War had on Britain's class system. Just as Churchill, himself an aristocrat, had to draw on the best brains, regardless of class, to help win the war, so the comparably aristocratic FDR had to do the same, regardless of ethnic origins and religion – not yet race – to fight the Depression. Both experiences, by revealing the anachronistic narrowness of the two countries' respective ruling classes, led to the broadening of the social base, not so much in the name of social or racial equality as of national efficiency. The aim, however, as much for FDR as for Churchill, was not to replace the old ruling order, or even to dilute it, but rather to strengthen it by cooption. That, at least in the American case, was its effect: the Wasp ascendancy was still in fine fettle when next I visited the United States as a *Times* Washington correspondent in 1951; in far finer fettle, as it happened, than the old ruling class in London, which had not yet recovered its nerve after the effects of the Labour party landslide in 1945.

And what a joy it was to be in Washington in those post-war years – described subsequently by Dean Acheson, then Secretary of State, as like being 'in at the creation' (of the post-war NATO Alliance) – but to be young was very heaven.* The Whig–Liberal wing of the Wasp aristocracy, which had responded in the 1930s to FDR's appeal to come to Washington to help rescue the Republic from the Depression, was still in charge, under his much less grand but nevertheless Wasp successor President Truman – resembling Abraham Lincoln at least in this respect. The most prominent of them, known as 'the six wise men' (Dean Acheson, Bob Lovett, Paul Nitze, Averill Harriman, John

---

* In his memoirs, my friend and colleague Joe Alsop, himself a Wasp patrician, describes his bachelor apartment of the period in the following mouthwatering terms: 'My Washington house, though far from pretentious, was extremely generous for a rent of $125 a month. I could have twelve, at a pinch fourteen, people for dinner. I had a permanent manservant, a wonderful Filipino ... whom I recruited straight from a Washington taxi cab and paid $25 a week to cook, clean, wash, press linen, and wait at table. Add to this a beautiful garden, a big living room, a large library, a decent dining room, and a big bedroom-dressing room and bath ...' This, mind you, was before his days as a world-famous columnist.

McCloy, and George Kennan), mostly close friends from the same Ivy League universities and sharing the same Roman Republican virtues, were in effect determining the shape of the post-war world. Nor were the six wise Wasp grandees at the top unrepresentative, since the State Department at that time was able to boast of being able 'to field a whole baseball team' of Harvard alumni ambassadors, including a Cabot, a Lodge, a Dillon, and an Aldrich, which is a bit as if London's post-Ernest Bevin Foreign Office – by then long resigned to playing down its aristocratic image – had suddenly gone mad and found it appropriate to boast about having on its ambassadorial roll call a Scrope, a Percy, a Howard, and a Russell.

The insensitivity of Wasp arrogance quite took my breath away, Dean Acheson's in particular. Over six feet tall and ramrod straight, he reminded me quite startlingly of the last of the great English pro-consuls, 'the very superior' first Marquis Curzon of Kedleston, and not only physically since the two of them shared a patrician manner of studied pro-vocativeness. For example, I remember Acheson, when up before the House Un-American Activities Committee, who were all shouting at him at the same time, giving great offence by requesting, with patrician politeness, that his tormentors should first put up their hands before asking any further questions.

Being a *Times* correspondent, which carried with it an honorary Wasp status, and a friend of the famous columnists Joe and Stewart Alsop (the last of whom had volunteered to serve in the British Army in 1939), I was allowed to sit in on the fringes of that world – attend the same George-town dinner parties and country-house weekends and take part in the same high political talk. It was rather as life must have been for a young member of Milner's kindergarten returning to London from South Africa to help in the running of the British Empire. Of course non-Wasps were not entirely excluded – any more than non-aristocrats, like John Buchan, were excluded from the Milner kindergarten. Felix Frankfurter, only the second Jewish Supreme Court Judge, for example, presided as its resident sage. Nevertheless, the accepted style, to which all the new recruits had to conform, was unmistakably upper-class Ivy League Wasp; and so powerful was this compulsion that the internationally famous publicist and journalist Walter Lippmann (also very much a central figure in the circle, as he had also been in the Roosevelt crowd) never dared to write about the Nazi persecution of the Jews lest by drawing attention to his own membership of that race he might jeopardize his cherished membership of the exclusive Metropolitan Club, from which Jews were still barred.

As for an aristocracy, in post-war Washington there was one operating at full throttle, to the immense benefit, I would say, of the whole world.

It was, however – as I should have remembered from my prewar experience of it in Maine – an aristocracy divided against itself. Shortly after my arrival in Washington in 1951, for example, Joe Alsop had invited me to dinner, only to ring up a day later to apologize – something he seldom did – for having failed to warn me that amongst the other guests would be the 'notorious' – his adjective – Republican Senate Leader, Robert Taft, son of President Taft. Under these circumstances, 'naturally', he would understand if I wanted to cancel. If it had been a London hostess of the same period telephoning to say that she would understand if I did not wish to sit down at the same table as Sir Oswald Mosley, or a French hostess to say she would understand if I did not wish to dine with a well-known collaborator, that would have been natural. But Senator Taft was not a traitor or a collaborator: he was a member of one of America's most prestigious families and the eminently respectable Wasp leader of America's 'loyal' Opposition. As such, he was someone whom a visiting journalist would naturally have been most particularly anxious to meet.

Just how vulnerable this bitter division rendered the Wasp aristocracy soon became clear when Joe McCarthy, an Irish Senator from the Wisconsin sticks, accused the 'silver spoon in mouth' Liberal-New Deal patrician wing of the Democratic Party of being 'soft on Communism'. But whereas the English Establishment of the period faced by the identical charge – with rather more justification – closed ranks, the American one fell apart. Driven to desperate tactics by having been kept out of power since 1932, the corporate East Coast–Wall Street wing of the Republican Party, including Robert Taft, tacitly backed the Irish Senator – whom none of them would ever have thought of receiving in their own mansions – thereby throwing their very considerable weight onto the side of the masses against the classes. Electorally it paid off. The Republicans under Eisenhower swept back into power in 1952, and, with that purpose achieved, swiftly and almost effortlessly put an end to McCarthyism – something that could have been done years earlier had not the two wings of the Wasp establishment been at each other's throats.

When the Senator did eventually fall, he fell like Lucifer never to rise again. By then, however, one felt almost sorry for him, so much the underdog had he become. Grotesquely overreaching himself, he had gone as far as accusing the army itself of being 'soft on Communism': no charge could have been more certain to close the Wasp ranks against him and to demonstrate how invincible those ranks, once united, still were. The line-up in the Congressional hearings that followed these allegations said it all. On the one side of the table sat the heavily jowled, slumped figure of the Irish Senator, flanked by a job lot of equally unappetizing upwardly mobile ethnics – with one exception they were all either Irish, Greek, Italian, or Jewish – and on the other, as far as the non-military spokesmen of the Eisenhower Administration went, all were clean-cut, well-scrubbed, square-jawed, Anglo-Saxon, East Coast patrician Protestants. It was no contest.

But by this time the damage had been done. Both wings of the Wasp ascendancy had come out badly from the McCarthy experience: the Whig–Liberal–New Deal Democratic patricians because of their appearance of unpatriotic under-reaction to the communist threat and the corporate Wall Street old-money Republicans because of their appearance of partisan over-reaction to it. Such behaviour served to cast doubt on what had been the Wasps' most valuable inheritance: their hitherto unchallenged freehold monopoly of a superior patriotism, a purer quality of Americanism than that belonging to any other ethnic group. As a serious politically radical movement designed to overthrow a patrician class of Wasps and replace it from below by a plebeian class of ethnics, McCarthyism never had a chance. With the Depression long since over and the 1950s boom in full swing, there were no material or economic issues going for it, and no united working class behind it; only a hotchpotch of grievances about social status, and it takes more than chips on shoulders to make a revolution. Even so, McCarthyism certainly succeeded in at least tarnishing the image of the old Wasp ruling class for ever. Before McCarthy the Wasps had been seen as the only authentic living embodiment of truly 'American activities'. After McCarthy an association with 'un-American activities' was never to be entirely erased. A spell had been broken.

So it was not really quite as much of a miracle as it seemed when five years later, in 1960, an Irish Catholic, J. F. Kennedy, with roots in the Boston southside (and whose brother Robert had been on McCarthy's staff), succeeded in getting himself elected President of the United States. By that time, however, the sleazy Senator himself was already dead and buried, which was just as well because there would certainly have been no place for the likes of him in Camelot.

It is always thus. Revolutions, like wars and everything else, have unintended consequences; and instead of the first

Catholic Irish–American President in the White House taking class out of the nation's capital as it might have been expected to do, class was put back in to a degree never before achieved even by George Washington – which is precisely what the Kennedy patriarch, Joseph Kennedy, had always intended. Being an uncultivated and philistine buccaneer himself, the last thing he wanted to leave behind was a family no better than himself. His express ambition was to found a new historic American dynasty – only this time an Irish one – that could compete with, and even out-shadow, all the great Wasp dynasties, like the Adams, the Cabots, the Lodges, the Peabodys, the Aldrichs, the Roosevelts, and the Tafts. Making money for him was never an end in itself. He is even on record as actually boasting that none of his children was in the least interested in making money. He had seen to that by ensuring that each of them was endowed with a fortune at birth, precisely so that they could feel free to serve the public interest, unburdened by the cares and fears of the common man. No Wasp patriarch would have dared to defy democratic sensitivities so brazenly. Democracy did not come into it; what Joseph Kennedy admired, and wanted to reproduce, was aristocracy, in the form of a family that could not only reach the top but also, and much more importantly, *stay there*; weave itself into the very fabric of the nation; in a word, institutionalize itself. Such an ambition went far beyond any previous Wasp aspiration. For whereas a traditional Wasp aspiration was to found a dynasty whose writ ran in a city – on a par, say, with Thomas Mann's Buddenbrooks or the Chamberlains

141

of Birmingham – Joseph Kennedy's was for a dynasty on a continental scale, more like Napoleon's. And just as Napoleon was a commoner who created a new royal dynasty, which even the grandest European aristocrats of that period would not have imagined themselves doing, so Joseph Kennedy was a non-Wasp who founded a dynasty with tentacles reaching from coast to coast, a feat beyond the aspirations of even the grandest of East Coast Wasp patricians. E. Digby Baltzell, in *The Protestant Establishment*, published soon after President Kennedy's assassination, explains how this aggrandizing project came to pass.

The Kennedys are not only a talented, prolific and independently wealthy political clan; they are also important, and of timeless significance, because of the fact that their extended family includes representatives of a wide variety of contemporary elites in this country: thus members of the Hollywood celebrity elite, so often rootless outcasts from the centers of stolid communal authority in America, are brought into the Kennedy establishment through the Peter Lawfords and their position at the heart of the Frank Sinatra 'clan'; the old stock upper class is represented in Sargent Shriver, Yaleman of an old Maryland family; and, of course, the late President's gifted wife, though born of Wall Street and Catholic wealth much like the Kennedys, is also the step-daughter of a member of old stock and Brown Stone New York which has been dissected so well in recent years by the author Louis Auchincloss.

Baltzell fails to mention that one of Joe Kennedy's daughters was also married to the Marquis of Hartington, heir to the Duke of Devonshire; or that Jackie Kennedy's sister was married to a Prince Radziwill, a very prominent émigré aristocrat with close connections to what remained of the *ancien régime* aristocracy on both sides of the Atlantic. In other words, the Kennedys were in a position to assimilate the members of a wide variety of contemporary elites, at any rate temporarily, into some sort of a new and stable establishment. Nor was this done unintentionally. For Jack Kennedy was always fascinated by England's Old Whig eighteenth- and nineteenth-century grandee families, under whose aegis old landed wealth had joined forces with new commercial wealth. So fascinated was he that Lord David Cecil's then famous book about the young Lord Melbourne, Queen Victoria's first prime minister, was his favourite bedside reading (not that he had all that much time for reading in bed*). One of the most thumbed passages, as we now know, went as follows:

A Whig Lord was so often as not a minister, his eldest son an MP, his second attached to a Foreign Embassy, so that their houses were alive with effort and hurry of politics . . . Whig society itself was a sort of club, exclusive, but in which those who managed to achieve membership lived on equal terms; a rowdy, rough and

---

* Richard Nixon's favourite bedtime reading, incidentally, was Robert Blake's *Disraeli*.

tumble club, full of conflict and plain speaking, where people were expected to stand up for themselves and give and take hard knocks ... Born and bred citizens of the world, they knew their way about it by a sort of infallible instinct. And they had an instinctive mastery of its social arts. Their negligence was never boorish; it arose from the fact that they felt so much at home in life that they were careless of its conventions ... For they possessed – it was their chief charm – in the highest degree, the high spirits of their home.

Nothing New England about that, for sure, and if a Roosevelt or an Adams had secretly dreamt of such a merry-monarch, cavalier approach to the business of public office, he would have kept such un-Puritan yearnings strictly to himself. No longer. Under the Kennedys this Whig style carried a kind of royal warrant. It was the official style to which the media were actively encouraged to bear witness (and I, for one, was very happy to comply), particularly during the Cuban Missile Crisis, which was a class act on a classic scale. But it was a class act with a noticeably different cast. For by the 1960s, thanks to the Ivy League universities' quota system, a whole new generation of Washington non-Wasp high-flyers – including the Kennedy brothers – had been fully integrated with their Wasp peers; integrated, that is, from Ivy League prep school age onwards. Wasp and non-Wasp high-flyers of that generation, including Jack Kennedy, had also been through the even more intense bonding process of serving together in positions of command on active wartime service.* Things had moved on since the days of the New Deal when FDR had plucked non-Wasps straight from the ranks, so to speak, to deal with the Depression; moved on, too, in the sense that while to FDR and Eleanor Roosevelt's generation non-Wasps would have been acceptable only as professional colleagues, to Kennedy's generation they were acceptable also as friends. Ethnic and religious distinctions, at least in Washington's corridors of power, had by then become almost meaningless. For the first time there was a truly heterogeneous American establishment.

Once again I was lucky enough to be well placed to note this social change. When the Cuban Missile Crisis broke, I was staying with an American journalist friend, a non-Wasp who during the Second World War had been an officer in the American Marine Corps (which, before the war, had been almost as much a private stamping ground for Wasp patricians as the Brigade of Guards had been for patrician Brits). Among his closest old classmates was one of President Kennedy's senior Wasp advisers who had been with the President in the White House throughout the crisis. It had been a hair-raising time and on the day the Russians blinked, bringing the crisis to an end, he and several other of Kennedy's lieutenants – including a Jew – came to dinner.

---

* The Second World War had had something of a similar effect in England. Freddie Ayer once told me that he had left Eton still a 'Jew boy' but by the time he had served as an officer in the wartime Welsh Guards he had been genuinely accepted as an English gentleman: a natural member of the ruling class.

All of them had known each other from childhood, and they gave us a rundown of what had happened – who had been the doves and who the hawks, etc. What I remember best is not my pleasure at being vicariously in on the act, so to speak, but the way these American patricians – for the first time non-Wasps as much as Wasps – took their centre-stage roles in the making of history as being nothing out of the ordinary, just part of what, as American patricians, they had been born to – rather as the Duke of Wellington's Old Etonian commanders would have done after defeating Napoleon at Waterloo.

The day after the dinner party I attended Kennedy's victorious White House press conference, his first public appearance since he had gone into seclusion for the duration of the crisis. The great auditorium was overflowing with newsmen from all over the world, for once more anxious to pay homage than to ask questions. When the President strode in from the wings everybody stood up and cheered. Many were in tears. Perhaps it was only in our imagination that the President seemed to have grown in stature. As I put it in a starstruck dispatch: 'before the crisis he had been a glamorous Prince Hal; now he was every inch a King . . . more, even every inch the Emperor of the West'. Hyperbole, of course; but whereas all previous presidents would have been embarrassed, not to say insulted by such royal and imperial comparisons, particularly coming from the pen of an English journalist, this, the first non-Wasp president, took them as his natural due. Irony of ironies: it had taken an Irish–American president to feel at home wearing the imperial purple – something even George Washington, although sorely tempted in his old age, had never dared to do.

Camelot did not last, of course, and the likelihood of there ever being a Kennedy III gets less attractive and more remote with every passing year. But what I did not realize at the time was that Camelot – by which I mean that symbolic moment in history when non-Wasp Americans proved their leadership mettle and took up their rightful position centre stage – had resulted in large measure from a conscious act of social engineering undertaken by the Wasps, the express purpose of which was not so much to serve the best interests of the ethnic minorities as to secure the best interests of Uncle Sam. It happened like this. Towards the end of the Second World War, once victory was assured, it began to dawn on the Wasp establishment that the role of the USA in the last half of the twentieth century would be incomparably more onerous than it had ever been before: nothing less than to undertake the burden of world leadership that had previously rested on the shoulders of Great Britain. For this enormously expanded role there would be required a cadre of public-spirited national leaders greatly beyond the capacity of the traditional Wasp leadership class to supply. What could be done about this became the burning question of the hour. As chance had it, the then president of Harvard, Dr James B. Conant, happened to be a man of controversially advanced liberal views who had long sought ways of opening up the Ivy League universities to ethnic talent far beyond the confines allowed by the old quota system. He saw in this new national emergency opportunities for promoting this ideal in a way likely to overcome the objections not only of his own conservative-minded governing body, but also of the equally conservative-minded governing bodies of all the other Ivy League universities. Egalitarian ideals alone, he well knew, would never be sufficient to persuade them to open up their doors more than a chink. But perhaps the new need to open them up in the urgent national interest would prove more persuasive. So, in a series of vastly influential articles and books, he set about propagating the idea that it was the duty of the Ivy League universities, in the last half of the twentieth century and in the public interest, to undertake the task of furnishing the American Empire with a meritocracy, rather as the great Dr Jowett, the famous Master of Balliol College, Oxford, had done for the British Empire in the last half of the nineteenth century.

While engaged in this great campaign of persuasion, however, Dr Conant, to his delight, came upon a quotation from Thomas Jefferson, the iconic author of the Declaration of Independence, which he rightly regarded as ideal grist to his mill – as certain to disarm his critics on the Right, because of its conservative-sounding language, as his critics on the Left, because of its author's impeccably liberal democratic credentials.

In a letter to John Adams, his presidential predecessor, Thomas Jefferson had written:

I agree with you that there is a natural aristocracy among men. The grounds of this are virtue and talent . . . The natural aristocracy I consider as the most precious gift of nature for the instruction, the trusts and the government of society ... May we not even say that that form of government is the best which provides the most effectually for as pure selection of these natural aristoi into the offices of government?

'Selection of natural aristoi into the offices of government' – that was precisely what the Ivy League universities must now do; and this meant replacing the self-indulgent sons of rich Wasp alumni who only went to university for the fun and games, with no intention of going on into public service – and who better than a president of Harvard to know how many of these there were? – with the more talented and virtuous sons of less privileged ethnic minorities who, in return for the privilege of an Ivy League university education, would almost certainly want to pay back their debt to society by going into the public service.

All the emphasis was on creating a leadership class – explicitly, in Jefferson's immortal words, 'a natural aristocracy'. Giving equal opportunities to the ethnic minorities was certainly a part of the purpose. Just as, in the early days, all Americans had had the opportunity to make it by acquiring land out West, so henceforth in the post-war world they would have the opportunity to make it by acquiring an East Coast Ivy League university degree. But what made the project so irresistible to all the anglophile Ivy League governing bodies was its classical appeal to their republican sense of pride and duty.

Thus it was that the idea of aristocracy, which, as I have tried to indicate, was always lurking in the American under-growth, came, quite late in the day, into the open; dragged out, moreover, by a famously liberal and progressive President of Harvard who could not possibly be accused of harbouring reactionary sentiments. For what Conant was advocating, he made clear, was not the rescue of some clapped-out idea of Old World aristocracy from the dustbin of history but the creation of a strikingly new, modernized, all-American type of New World aristocracy. His was not a backward looking idea; quite the opposite. It was a positively revolutionary idea. Henceforth not only should every American have the right to life, liberty, and the pursuit of happiness but also the right to have a go at becoming, in Jefferson's phrase, 'a natural aristocrat'.* Yes, there were going to be degrees, but not degrees of nobility – the dreaded dukes and earls, etc.; rather degrees of worth and talent – BAs, MAs, PhDs. The word 'pedigree' itself was to be given a new meaning.

Nor did Dr Conant rest content with articulating a gen-eral principle; he also went on to describe the social engin-eering method to give it substance.† Intelligence tests, which had been widely used in the war for officer selection,

---

* Here, of course, the distinction between aristocracy and meritoc-racy becomes blurred. But it is interesting to note that Conant himself did not hesitate to use the word aristocracy.
† See Nicholas Lemann's groundbreaking *The Big Test: The Secret History of the American Meritocracy* (New York: Farrar, Straus and Giroux, 1999), which gives a critical account of this extraordinary project to create an American governing class.

should be used. After much refining – he argued – a new system of such tests could do the same kind of job for civilians in peace time. The idea was to use all the latest testing techniques to evaluate every American high school student by a single national standard and then to make sure that they went to the colleges most suited to their abilities and ambitions. Here again, however, a quotation about aristocracy from another American icon, Ralph Waldo Emerson,* came usefully to hand. For in his famous essay on aristocracy Emerson had argued very forcefully that a society had every right to grade its citizens 'according to their weight and value', putting the superior above the inferior with 'every adult citizen placed where he belongs'. 'It must be agreed everywhere', he wrote, 'that every society must have the benefit of the best leaders.' Very regretfully, however, Emerson had conceded that 'in the absence of such an anthroponeter' there was no way of scientifically drawing up such an order of merit. For that reason alone, therefore, aristocracy had to be ruled out as an impractical ideal. Not any longer, retorted Conant. Seizing on Emerson's concession that, in principle, 'those eminent by personal qualities should enjoy proper influence', he argued that, unlike in Emerson's day, the intelligence tests constituted exactly such 'an anthroponeter' capable of putting the principle into practice. In other words, the American aristocracy, unlike all previous aristocracies, would have a

---

* In volume II of the *Complete Works of Ralph Waldo Emerson* published by Wm. H. Wise, New York 1929.

scientific basis. Instead of being an aristocracy of the past, it would be an aristocracy of the future. Henceforth every American high school student should be evaluated by the same testing techniques and sent to colleges best suited to their ability. Only in this way, he concluded, would the United States get a leadership class of a size and quality fit to fulfil its post-war destiny. Such was Conant's influence and persuasive power in the circles that mattered – the Ivy League universities and their old alumni in high circles in Washington – that his plan was adopted with astonishing speed – the Cold War was looming – and put into practice, bringing about in the last half of the twentieth century what has amounted to a radical change in the American social structure.

What a contrast with how Britain, during the identical period, was planning to cope with the challenges of the postwar world. While the president of Harvard and the American establishment were plotting and planning for America to rise to those challenges by creating a 'natural aristocracy', the then director of the London School of Economics, William Beveridge, another controversial liberal, was plotting and planning for Britain to do so by creating a welfare state. While Britain was putting its faith in the masses, America was putting its faith in the elites. How Tocqueville would have cheered. He had always prophesied that America would give aristocracy a new lease of life and now he was being proved right. Democracy understood as a fairer system for recruiting into an aristocracy: that was henceforth to be the American way forward.

After over half a century of vigorous and thorough implementation, how has Dr Conant's system of selection (Scholastic Aptitude Tests or SATs) worked out? In one sense, its aim has been triumphantly achieved: the idle and dissolute members of the old Wasp ruling class have been dethroned, and the brightest and best of the new ethnic groups put in their place. Jefferson's dream of a selective process able to secure 'worth and genius from every condition of American life' has been implemented, even to some degree in the case of the blacks. Unfortunately, however, this aristocracy of natural talent – brainpower tested by competitive examinations – turned out, at any rate at first, to contain even more backsliders, in one crucial sense, than had the old Wasp aristocracy. For in Conant's dreams all the new class of first-generation, highly educated 'natural aristocrats', drawn from every walk of life and background, should have possessed, as not all the old Wasp aristocrats did, the best qualities of aristocracy – a sense of public duty and civic virtue – without any of the vices endemic in an hereditary aristocracy – idleness, immorality, and luxurious tastes. Not having been born to take a privileged education for granted, they could not fail, he believed, to accept the obligation to put a lot back. So the process of broadening out the entry to Ivy League universities to include all the best and brightest among the ethnic groups would simply mean, he assumed, more Jewish, Catholic, black and brown Achesons, Roosevelts and Harrimans.

Unfortunately it didn't quite work out like that. For what the first- and second-generation of American natural aristocrats, without any private means, turned out to want were the material advantages – access, that is, to the well-paid corporate jobs that went with an Ivy League education – without at the same time producing out of their ranks the required quota of civic leaders: they wanted the palm without the dust. Not that the new men were in any way idle; but success in their eyes was measured more by getting to the top than by what they did for the Republic once at the top, which is scarcely surprising since, unlike the hereditary Wasp aristocrats who had been able to sail through higher education with relatively little effort, competing only with their social equals, the new meritocrats had to work their guts out to compete against the best of the brains of the whole population – a very much more arduous experience that produced leaders for whom altruism only came at an almost impossibly high price.

The trouble was that Dr Conant's idea of the effects of university education had not kept up with reality. In the nineteenth and early parts of the twentieth century, the assumption had been that going to a university was a great hindrance when it came to the business of making money. Few of the legendary tycoons or robber barons – Andrew Carnegie, for example – had been to university; some scarcely even to school. That, they were fond of boasting, was their good fortune. Higher education would have been more a handicap than a launching pad. Instead of sharpening the edge of competitive avarice, it tended to blunt it. So it would never have occurred to Dr Conant that by sending anyone to university he might be turning their eyes towards the service of Mammon. He took it for granted that he was turning their eyes, if not to God, then at least to higher things.

Although partially true once, this was no longer true at all after 1945. For by then advances in science and technology had introduced such complexity into pretty well every aspect of business and commerce as to make a high level of education almost a necessary condition of success. Sheer willpower, native wit, and raw greed were no longer of much avail without high levels of intellect and expertise. So after the Second World War, far from higher education rendering young men unfit for business and commerce, it had started to render them ideally suited for business and commerce. So it is no wonder that Dr Conant's great post-war exercise in social engineering, designed to give the best and brightest Americans from all backgrounds greater opportunities to serve in government and public life, ended up by giving them greater opportunities to corner the riches of America for themselves – a development that may well have done wonders for the American economy but was almost the exact opposite of what the good doctor ordered.

This being America, however, there was no inhibition on the part of the respectable academic and intellectual community about discussing quite calmly the possibility that the replacement of the historic Wasp aristocracy by a new first-generation of careerists from unprivileged backgrounds might have been a great mistake – not, of course, from the point of view of the new careerists themselves, whose opportunities had been enormously expanded, but from that of the national interest.

Having been in the USA a lot in the late 1950s and early 60s, I remember this debate very well, if only because the regrets being expressed in respectable intellectual circles about the dissolution of the old Wasp Establishment contrasted so strikingly with the criticism being expressed in the same circles in England about the survival of the old English Establishment. This suited me well enough because whereas in England my strong inclination to defend the old order put me completely outside the prevailing intellectual fashion (it made me virtually unemployable by the BBC, for instance), in New York it made me quite a hot property – written up, for example, in *Time* magazine and taken up by the *New Yorker*, then as now a reliable barometer of intellectual fashion.

Regrets about the disappearance of the old Wasp ascendancy were not in any way limited to Southern conservatives or right-wing fanatics. The most articulate expression of these doubts came from a new generation of New York Jewish intellectuals – notably Ed Shils, Dan Bell, Irving Kristol and his wife Gertrude Himmelfarb, all of whom were soon to become internationally famous. Most surprising of all, even James Baldwin, the radical black novelist, then at the height of his fame, also waxed nostalgic about the end of the Wasp ascendancy, as the following moving quotation makes clear:

I suppose it can be said that there was a time in this country when an entity existed . . . let us say a class, for the lack of a better word, which created the standards by which America lived or which created the standards to which America aspired. I am referring to or have in mind, perhaps somewhat arbitrarily, the aristocracies of Virginia and New England. These were mainly of Anglo-Saxon stock and they created what Henry James was to refer to, not very much later, as our Anglo-American heritage, or Anglo-American connection. Now at no time did these men ever form anything resembling a popular majority. Their importance was that they kept alive and they bore witness to two elements of a man's life which are not greatly respected among us now: (1) the social forms, called manners, which prevent us from rubbing too abrasively against one another and (2) the interior life, the life of the mind.

Something valuable had gone missing, and sensitive Americans were feeling the loss. One article in particular has stuck in my mind. It was written by a don at Cornell University, Andrew Hacker, and appeared in a 1957 number of the prestigious *American Political Science Review*, which I have by me as I write. It described the wounds dealt to the American body politic by the destruction of the Wasp ascendancy with an unflinching clarity that would have been unthinkable in any equivalent British academic journal considering the destruction of the class system in England. The article started by declaring flatly that a society that encourages the full flowering of individual liberty has to be socially stratified; has to have a class at the top secure enough in its position to risk resisting popular demands for infringements of individual liberty. Not that they championed individual liberty exclusively for the sake of that ideology's own intrinsic virtue, or for the purpose of giving the mass of the community an opportunity to develop their potentiality. Rather, the idea of a limited government was for their own class benefit. The reasons for this, on the economic side – laissez-faire – were obvious. But in the process of pursuing these economic advantages, the Wasp ascendancy had come to defend the Bill of Rights, the common law, and the whole idea of decency, civility and fair play – in short, the framework of liberal democracy. The judges and lawyers who came from this class were willing to interpret the constitution in such a way that dissenters would be allowed free rein to express their thoughts. This tolerance, however, did not come from any abstract love for civil liberties. It was simply that the ruling class itself counted *among its own members* individuals who possessed radical views and who tended to display idiosyncratic behaviour. In order to protect its own kind, it was prepared to give strength to the law by ensuring that the Bill of Rights was a living doctrine.

For almost a century and a half, Hacker writes, America had had just such a leisured class:

To be sure, many of its members toiled mightily in the vineyards. But their upbringing and even their adult years were devoid of the pressures imposed on the new men of today. That leisure enabled them to study, not necessarily in a formal, but often in a disciplined way – responsibilities and obligations which were to be theirs. The lawyer had, of course, to serve his client. But he was able to serve the common law and the constitution at the same time. In short, men of leisure were able to regard their power as an instrument for transmitting traditional values as well as an instrument for performing particular tasks at hand. These values were sustained by a class which could ignore the demands of career building and organizational competition. For it is plain enough that there is all too frequently a conflict between, let us say, defending the Bill of Rights and earning a dollar or winning a vote. Simple exhortation is not enough to lead a man to strike a blow for the one at the risk of losing the other. He must first be sure that he is in a position to make a short run sacrifice for the long term good.

The new men are not cushioned either by status or by private income. If we ask the newly arrived man – who, let it be said, is never completely sure that he has arrived – to take a stand on fundamental liberties, we are asking too much of him. One may, with good reason, demand this of a senator from an old Cincinnati family or of a Boston lawyer of wealth and standing to stake a claim in defence of the First Amendment. But to ask this of a bright young politician from California or an engineer who has risen through the ranks of an automobile company is asking the impossible.

Asking the impossible. Ominous words, because the main reason, as I indicated earlier, for Tocqueville's faith in American democracy had been that it was possible to ask 'the impossible' of its professional and middle classes; that it was possible to expect the American middle class to put the good of the country before their own personal interests; was possible, that is, for the American middle class and professional class to fill the gap at the top of a society left by the absence of an aristocracy. That was in the early nineteenth century, during the unchallenged Wasp ascendancy. But by 1957, Hacker argued, the Wasp ascendancy, having been replaced in the interests of national efficiency by a new lot of top dogs much more vulnerable to populist pressure, these liberal principles – except as regards laissez-faire – would be in much more serious danger.

From today's perspective, however, perhaps the most interesting part of Hacker's 1957 article is that it concluded with a prophecy. He prophesised that America's new men, no longer able to command automatic deference, would soon have to develop an alternative system of control: psychic manipulation, the techniques of which, he warned, were even then being perfected. So into the vacuum created by the end of deference would flow a new political system of control called 'public relations', which could best be described as the art of leading while claiming not to lead, and of giving orders to the people while pretending to be taking orders from them. Again, the contrast with the 1957 debate in Britain was pretty stark. For while Britain's Anthony Crosland was agonizing about *The Future of*

Socialism, his progressive counterparts and friends in the United States were agonizing, in effect, about the loss of aristocracy.

By the end of the twentieth century, however, with the new men in America no longer so new, there was a very different story to tell – a story no longer of the destructive consequences of the disappearance of an *old-money* hereditary ruling class but of the constructive consequences of the arrival of an *old-brains* hereditary ruling class. Again there has been no lack of respectable American academics and intellectuals willing to chronicle, and even celebrate, this new development, pointing out that after more than fifty years of selecting only the very brainy for the benefit of higher education – and after almost as long of an information-age economy that offers its best financial rewards to the highly intelligent – there had been time enough for a new kind of very American patrician to emerge: a new kind of superior person who was not only at once impressively brainy and impressively successful at making money, but also, more often than not, the sons and daughters or the grandsons and granddaughters of parents and grandparents who had similar qualities. Of course the old Wasp ruling class had not lacked intellectual and cultivated elements; but whereas in their case these elements were the cherry on the cake, in the case of the new class these brainy ingredients were very much the money-making cake itself. Increasingly, therefore, braininess and cultivation were becoming the qualities to which the mass of Americans were now beginning to look up. Moreover, while the first generation of beneficiaries of SATs in the information age, in the 1960s, had been radical and bloody-minded, concerned only to destroy the Wasp morality – particularly sexual morality – and Puritan values, the second and third generations were more concerned to create new rules and customs, a new sexual morality, and even, *mirabile dictu*, a new tradition of public service. But because each successive generation of this new ruling class, in turn, had to face the dreaded SAT challenge – instead of being able to rely, as their Wasp predecessors had, on inheritance to ease their way into the Ivy League universities – its slackers and idlers got weeded out. So it was a ruling class, indeed increasingly an hereditary ruling class – that was kept on its toes, ever mindful of the need to continue to prove its worth: aristocracy, that is, at its best.

This development is brilliantly portrayed by David Brooks in his book *Bobos in Paradise*, Bobos being his way of describing a new amalgam between bohemians and bourgeoisie. According to Mr Brooks:

It includes artists who, by founding design firms, have discovered a way to pursue their muse and still qualify for stock options; by *bon viveur* bankers who, by building gourmet companies like Ben and Jerrys or Nan Tucket Nectars, have found a way to be hippy dippies and multi-national corporate cats; by advertising copywriters who, by using William S. Burroughs ads for Nike sneakers and incorporating Rolling Stone anthems in their marketing campaigns, have reconciled

the anti-establishment style with the corporate imperative; by stockbrokers who, dressing like Bill Gates in worn
chinos on the way to a stockholders' meeting, have reconciled undergraduate fashion with upper crust occupation; and by businessmen generally who, by going on
eco-adventure vacations, have reconciled aristocratic
thrill-seeking with social concern, and by shopping at
Benetton or the Boy Shop they have brought together
consciousness-raising and cost control.

This new establishment, which has crushed the old WASP
culture and now sits atop many of the same institutions that
their fathers or grandfathers in the 1960s once railed against,
has, Mr Brooks goes on to argue, begun to create a set of
social codes which gives a coherent structure to national
life.

Today, America once again has a dominant class that
defines the perimeters of respectable opinion and
taste – a class that determines conventional wisdom,
that promulgates a code of good manners, that estab-
lishes a pecking order to give shape to society, that
excludes those who violate its codes, that transmits its
moral and etiquette codes down to its children, that
imposes social discipline on the rest of society so as to
improve the 'quality of life', to use the contemporary
phrase.

This new establishment has assumed this role hesi-
tantly. It hasn't become a technocratic elite with a

strong sense of public service,* as many of the early champions of the meritocracy envisioned. It hasn't established clear lines of authority, since it still has trouble coming to terms with authority. Instead, it has exercised its influence through a million and one private channels, reforming society through culture more than through politics. Its effort to establish order have been spotty and often clumsy – all the political correctness codes, the speech codes on campuses, the sexual harassment rule. But gradually a shared set of understandings and practices has cohered into a widely accepted social norm. Thirty years ago, when tearing down the established structure was the order of the day, civility was not a cherished value, especially on campuses. But now that a new civil order has come into being, the word *civility* is again heard on nearly every educated person's tongue. And somehow some sort of looser social peace is in the process of being restored. Many of the social indicators that sky-rocketed during the age of transition, the 1960's and 1970's, have begun to drop: crime rates, abortion rates, illegitimacy, divorce rates, teenager drinking.

In effect, therefore, if not in intention, Mr Brooks concludes, this reconciliation between bourgeois and bohemian

---

* Brooks was writing in the Clinton years, but there would seem to be much evidence that in response to the challenges of international terrorism, and under the presidency of George W. Bush, a new leadership elite with a strong sense of public service is beginning to emerge, perhaps all too visibly.

values and lifestyles has produced a 'gently' authoritative upper class that emphatically does serve the common weal, even if the old Wasp Bostonian puritan aristocracy would not recognize or approve of it.

Any ambitious State exercise of power, like a new war on poverty, is out; so are big cities, big trusts, big bureaucracy or New Deals. The aim is more to take the lead in the exercise of what Mr Brooks describes as 'intimate' authority, in the family and in local communities – in what Burke used to call 'the little platoons'. Even so, the Bobos with their PhDs do go into national politics in Washington, furnishing Congress with most of its highly paid political aides, and into city politics, having completely replaced, in the running of the political parties, the old-style immigrant machine politicos. The days of the hard-drinking, blue-collared journalist are also over, as becomes obvious nowadays at a presidential press conference when the rows are filled by young Ivy League graduates.

Very possibly Mr Brooks paints an exaggerated picture of this new Bobo Whig-style aristocracy, which he makes seem a bit too good to be true. But the very fact that a fashionable journalist – who writes about culture regularly for the *New Yorker* – should want to dwell so admiringly on the existence throughout contemporary America of this new patrician class is relevant to the point I am seeking to make, which is not so much that America actually has a new upper class as that, increasingly, it is politically correct to take it for granted that the existence of such a sophisticated and cultivated class is a good idea; that its existence in the professions, corporations, foundations, publishing houses, and even armed forces, no less than in the universities and arts, enormously improves the quality of life for the nation as a whole, not only in the rich suburbs but also, to a greater or a lesser extent, among the population generally. What is more, for the first time in history, this task of spreading sweetness and light, raising levels of taste, and determining moral standards in public and private life is no longer in the un-American hands of a leisured, over-educated egg-head class. In the information age it has become a dynamic part of American *business* itself.

For what it is worth, my own experience suggests that Mr Brooks is on to something. For whenever I go to restaurants in London and find myself pleasantly surprised by the civilized conversational level, and by the attractive and stylish clothes being worn at the adjacent tables, those responsible always turn out to be Americans. Likewise when I go swimming in my expensive Thames-side country club – whose members are mostly drawn from Thames Valley residents – and notice, to my delight, an elegant blonde stretched out on her chaise longue reading Kafka, she too is invariably an American. Again, in my experience, the people who speak the best English on the *Today* programme, and the people who look and sound most civilized on television and radio programmes generally, are also almost always American (occasionally European, but almost never British). It never used to be so. It used to be the Americans who looked and sounded common. No longer. Today they seem and sound to be the only people who deserve an upward glance – an impression confirmed by my visits to America itself. Whereas in Henry James's day, sophisticated Americans came to Britain to experience a superior quality of life in all its aspects, today it would make more sense for sophisticated Brits in search of the same, to go to America.*

None of the above should be taken as disparaging America's justified claim to be the world's greatest democracy. It should be taken as adding strength to that claim by showing how a democracy can be strengthened by embracing – albeit very half-heartedly – the principle of aristocracy†, instead of – as is increasingly the case in Britain – weakened by trampling it underfoot.

---

* Whether this will survive the war against terrorism remains to be seen.

† This hot-cold American approach to *noblesse oblige* is beautifully captured in a report in the *Daily Telegraph* of 19 February, 2004, under the headline 'Brideshead night at Yale led Kerry to war'. At the height of the Vietnam war, according to the report, John F. Kerry, then an undergraduate at Yale University, was rooming with 'a scion of the Boston Brahmin aristocracy, Harvey Bundy' when his uncle, William Bundy, who had been a senior official in President Kennedy's State Department, called in 'for a few beers and, more importantly, to ask the gilded youth of Yale if they would fight for their country in Vietnam. Shortly afterwards, Mr Kerry enlisted in the navy, the service of his hero John F. Kennedy. Recounting this story, however, Harvey Bundy felt it necessary to deny that the evening was a meeting of aristocrats. 'My uncle wasn't appealing to us as children of privilege. It was more an appeal to duty and *leadership*.' [my italics].

Bill Bundy, son-in-law of Dean Acheson, incidentally, was one of the guests at the aforementioned celebratory dinner party in Washington I attended for those who had played a leading role in the Cuban Missile Crisis.

Five

'If you must marry an Englishman, make sure he is a gentleman.'

> General de Gaulle, to the eighteen year old Claude
> Bertrand de Colasse, who in the war served under
> him in the Free French, first in London and then in
> Algiers, she being the shortest member and he being
> the tallest of that splendidly ill-assorted company. In
> the event, before obeying his command by marrying
> me, she first married a Battle of Britain hero who
> happened to be Welsh.

England now passed, to her great good fortune, under the sway of a race that could teach her how to obey.

> Sir John Fortescue, Historian of the British Army,
> on the blessings accruing to England through
> the Norman Conquest.

If the United States should familiarize us to the idea of merchants and businessmen as aristocrats, France should do the same for the idea of bureaucrats and administrators as aristocrats. Here again an historical abridgement may help to make this point.*

---

* Here I have taken as my guide *The Idea of France* by Pierre Birnbaum (New York: Hill and Wang, 2001).

Determined to centralize all power in his own hands, Louis XIV, in the seventeenth century, used lawyers and civil servants – drawn from the ranks of the bourgeoisie – to wrest power out of the hands of the old feudal aristocratic class, conferring upon the haute bourgeoisie an aura of courtly glamour and distinction that, through different epochs and political regimes, they have retained to this day. Naturally the bourgeoisie welcomed this change, which in effect amounted to the replacement of hereditary aristocracy by bourgeois functionaries governing in the King's name. But for good reason their welcome was only partial. For while depriving *ancien régime* aristocrats of their powers, local and national, the King left them in possession of their feudal privileges – such as the right to carry arms and not to pay taxes – thereby guaranteeing that aristocrats henceforth aroused maximum hatred and minimal respect. It was a recipe for bourgeois revolution, which, in 1789, duly came. But it was a strange revolution. For the aim of the bourgeois functionaries was not so much to transfer power from the old aristocracy into their own hands – since that had already, to a large extent, been done – but to transfer the privileges that went with power to themselves, or at any rate to deprive the aristocrats of them. For since the bourgeois bureaucrats were now carrying aristocratic burdens and fulfilling aristocratic duties, surely it was only fair that they should enjoy aristocratic privileges as well. What the French revolutionaries were raging against, therefore, was not an aristocracy proper but a travesty of an aristocracy, an aristocracy that served no purpose, that took a lot in the way of unearned privilege and gave nothing back. They were raging not so much against the presence of aristocracy as its absence; not so much against nobility as, in a word, *ignobility*; and it was this ignobility – an aristocracy *manqué* reduced to the contemptible role of pampered parasites – that they hated, and hated far more than ever they loved freedom.

Nobility, in short, was precisely what the revolutionaries yearned for: a regenerated republican nobility. Revolutionary art and rhetoric made constant reference to the need for heroic deeds and grandiose thoughts. Any idea that the revolution had much to do with the common or the little man is almost literally wide of the mark.* When the revolutionaries talked of 'the citizen', they had in mind someone dedicated to the public service, more concerned to steer the ship of state than to paddle his own canoe, and more concerned with public than private business. 'Citizen' was a high title, an honorific, almost a military rank, carrying with it implications that, in reality, had much more to do with aristocratic duties than the rights of man. By 'citizen' the French revolutionaries meant 'active citizen', not so much an important individual in his own right as a self-sacrificial leader of an important nation. That, as they saw it, was the trouble with parliamentary government and liberal democracy: neither of those systems could be guaranteed

---

* In a famous text of 7 November 1793, the painter Jacques-Louis David proposed to the Convention that a gigantic monument of Hercules be constructed in the heart of Paris, symbolizing the French people as 'a race of giants'. See Birnbaum, *The Idea of France*, 67.

to produce men and women of a high enough quality to fulfil the revolutionary ideal. For that great revolutionary and regenerational purpose nothing short of heroic leaders were needed.

This, of course, was the mirror image of the high ideals set for France by Louis XIV. Only by Crown and Church acting together would France be able to carry out its divinely sanctioned sacred mission to be the first among nations in the struggle to promote and defend the Catholic faith. The difference was that in the case of the French revolutionaries it was the universal secular religion of humanism, rather than Catholicism, that required the dedicated service of France's best and brightest. Democracy did not come into the republican mission any more than it did into the royalist and Catholic mission. Nor, in the English sense, did aristocracy. But nobility most certainly did – a republican nobility that was also understood as a republican priesthood. So exalted was the republican ideal that the main fear was that there would not be enough republicans in France to realize it. Kings and cardinals might have been grand enough to serve Catholicism; but for the new religion of humanity a finer quality of citizen would be required. Historians tend to associate France's republican tradition with Napoleon's meritocratic offer of '*la carrière ouvert aux talents*'. That is to underestimate it. For the republican ideal was not primarily aimed at releasing the energies of exceptionally ambitious individuals but rather to enable France to ascend the heights. That was the dream; but where were the republican heroes to help realize it?

To begin with there was only one answer to that question. Revolutionary republican France was at war, and what she needed most urgently were citizen generals, one of whom, Napoleon Bonaparte, after conquering all of Europe in the name of the Enlightenment, had himself crowned emperor and created a new hereditary nobility to help him run it. At this point that did not seem so much a betrayal of the republican ideal as its natural consequence. The abstract and universal ideals of 'Liberty, Equality, and Fraternity' were so lofty that great men of action on white horses in their pursuit did not seem at all out of place – not nearly so out of place as would have been democratically elected career politicians arguing the toss in a parliamentary chamber. In any case, Napoleon saw no reason not to put his own authoritarian and aristocratic stamp on the bureaucratic character of the state machine inherited from the *ancien régime*, completing in the process the destruction of local and regional autonomy that Louis XIV had begun; nor did much change during the restoration of the Bourbon and then Orleanist dynasties, or during the restoration of the Napoleonic dynasty, since the rule from the centre by civil servants and their agents, with historically well founded aristocratic pretensions, was a thick thread running through them all.

Not until the advent of the Third Republic in 1875 was there a serious attempt to establish a 'Republic of Individuals' – a republic, that is, favouring the legislature against the executive and parliamentary democracy against republican authoritarianism, all forms of authoritarianism – particularly the bloodiest kind experienced during the Commune in 1870 – having by then fallen, at any rate temporarily, under the deepest of shadows. Indeed under the Third Republic's constitution, the Chamber of Deputies emerged as supreme and entirely overshadowed the president. But almost immediately this experiment in the democratization of politics provoked the haute bourgeoisie republican elites, who dominated the higher reaches of the administration and staffed the ministerial *cabinets*, into contemptuous protest. The language used was openly aristocratic. Parliamentarians were described, for example, as having the culture of 'provincial vets', and from this period dated the stereotype of the *député* as a provincial windbag, usually from the Midi, good for nothing except electioneering and intrigue. This antagonism went far beyond mere disapproval. The words 'rottenest', 'disgust', 'decadence', 'nausea', 'revulsion', constantly recur. Republican France's destiny was too important to be left to the kind of ill-educated and second-rate populist politicians likely to emerge from the electoral process. Up to a point, of course, the haute bourgeoisie were fearful – as were all the bourgeoisies everywhere in the nineteenth century – of the threat posed by mass democracy to property. But in the case of the French bourgeoisie there were concerns – at any rate in the upper reaches – that transcended material matters. For it has to be constantly borne in mind that France's bourgeois functionaries – the successors, that is, of the original revolutionaries – owed their existence in the first place to Louis XIV and to the Court of Versailles, which is the reason why France's republican and revolutionary tradition cannot be separated from the aristocratic model of courtly society. Indeed given such courtly origins in the seventeenth century, it would have been surprising if they had not been quite as concerned to maintain their position at the top of the cultural and aesthetic, literary, and philosophical trees as at the top of the financial and economic trees. There was a particularity about the French bourgeois avant-garde since, in its higher reaches, as well as being heirs to all the usual material concerns, they had also inherited France's noble obligation to tutor the whole world in the art of living. So to the chain of greed and acquisitiveness, common to all bourgeois classes everywhere, must be added, in the case of the French bourgeoisie, that of intellectual arrogance. Plainly it stood to reason that no mere 'Republic of Individuals', all pursuing their different aims, could possibly do justice to such an exalted destiny. What was required instead was, in a phrase much used at the time, '*La Republique des Notables*'.*

Criticisms of the Third Republic coming from within the republican and revolutionary consensus were as nothing to those coming from without – from the reactionary and royalist circles that had never accepted the revolutionary settlement in the first place and never ceased to hope and pray for its complete reversal. For them, naturally, the establishment of the Third Republic, after the long interregnum

---

* Julian Jackson, *France: the Dark Years, 1940–1944* (Oxford: Oxford University Press, 2001), 44.

of the Restoration and the Second Empire years, came as a bitter disappointment, justifying a ferocious resurgence of anti-republican and counter-revolutionary rhetoric, some of it bordering on insurrection. What should be recalled in this respect is that the original French revolutionary rage, fired by the Enlightenment belief in reason, was against Catholicism, the 'superstitions' of which, in the revolutionary tradition, were inextricably associated with, and blamed for, all the evils of the *ancien régime*. In fact in many ways bishops and priests, none of whose powers had been removed by the King, were more hated than the secular noblemen, all of whose powers had been removed. Revolutionary cruelty, therefore, created even more churchmen than noblemen as victims, and this in turn had fired in France a uniquely ferocious countervailing Catholic rage against the Enlightenment and all its servants. So just as the revolutionaries in 1789, following Voltaire, longed to see the last aristocrat strangled by the entrails of the last priest, so, a hundred years on, did the Catholic counter-revolutionaries, following Joseph de Maistre and Charles Maurras (reactionary Voltaires), long to see an equally gory fate for the politicians and administrators of the Third Republic. Parliamentary politics stood no chance against this background of Franco-French civil war. If the republicans were to be true to their vision of a France incarnating rationalism and humanism, then there was no comfortable room for Catholics; and if Catholics were to be true to their vision of France as the Church's favourite daughter, there would be no comfortable room for republicans. Neither of these two visions, it is worth noting, envisaged France as a collection of individuals with diverse aims and purposes: both envisaged France as a united nation with only one purpose. In the one vision, the notables would be all Catholic and royalist, in the other all atheist and republican. No wonder the Third Republic was weak and indecisive. For although the constitution favoured parliamentary democracy, the prevailing ethos at the top was overwhelmingly in favour of something very different: rule by dedicated functionaries loyal to one or other of the two visions. Occasionally, as during the First World War, a parliamentary leader of the giant stature of Georges Clemenceau seemed to measure up to size; but for the most part, parliamentary politicians seemed an inferior breed, as foreign to the republican and rational idea of the nation as to the monarchical and Catholic idea.

Then came 1940 and the defeat of the Third Republic by German arms. In the event, however, it was no ordinary defeat since the great majority of republican functionaries, at any rate in unoccupied France, seemed quite happy to go on governing France under the First World War hero Marshal Pétain, with the enthusiastic co-operation of the Catholic and royalist counter-revolutionaries who thought their hour had struck. Because of the Vichy regime's treatment of the Jews it was a most shameful period. But in one way at least it was a blessing in disguise because during the Vichy years, for the first time since the Revolution, the pro-republican and the anti-republican elites, at all levels, started to feel able to work together. In particular, and of momentous importance, the Church was brought back into the national fold; not quite re-established but at least restored to a legitimate place in the governance of the country. Also reintegrated into governance were many of the old aristocratic families who had previously been held at arms-length, not so much because of their blue blood but because of their Catholic religion. True, this all happened under the watchful eye of the German conquerors, but happen it did, which meant that when peace came in 1945 old republican and old anti-republican foes shared a guilty secret: they had both collaborated. While not exactly transforming them into members of the same family, it at least turned them into partners in crime, all too aware that in the post-war future that lay ahead sticking together was the best way to avoid hanging separately. In this less than glorious way the Franco-French civil war was brought to an end. Unquestionably the Vichy years opened new wounds on France's body politic, but these did not cut nearly so deep as the old revolutionary wounds, which Vichy did so much to heal.

So although the Fourth Republic, established after the war, still had to carry the burden, like its predecessor, of French parliamentary parties and parliamentary government, it enjoyed one enormous advantage. It no longer contained, at any rate in metropolitan France, any significant elements of the old irreconcilably hostile forces of Catholic and monarchist reaction. The old spell cast by the two literary high priests of reaction, de Maistre and Maurras, had been broken. By the same token the anti-Catholic fires had also been extinguished in the ashes of defeat, as had the absolute certainties of the rule of reason. So for the first time since the Revolution, the State could plausibly claim to incarnate a united nation – even if the source of the new unity was largely a sense of guilt and shame common to both republicans and monarchists. The humiliations of Vichy had chastened the entire nation, shocking it into wanting to do better in future. For while on a superficial level the class war might seem to have been the sickness that so dolefully weakened the Third Republic's body politic, there was also a widespread realization, at a deeper level, that it was the nation's soul that most urgently needed purification.

One of the first tokens of this new resolve came with the setting up of a national school of public administration, the École nationale d'administration (ENA) – a new *grande école* (i.e. a super university) intended to mobilize a reunified citizenry in the public service not so much of the Republic – de Gaulle never sincerely used that word – as of the nation. Its express purpose was to recruit a higher quality of citizen into the public service, a task deemed to be very much more of a post-war priority than the provision of better education for the masses. This time, however, instead of discouraging the recruitment of Catholics, as would have happened under the Third Republic, they were welcomed, as were members of the old aristocracy. In this way the Fourth Republic made a valiant effort to reconnect France with its pre-revolutionary past; to start drawing national strength as much from the Cross as from the Tricolour; and to signal its determination in future to give an equally honoured place to spiritual values in the national life as to rational values. Something very similar was advocated by Solzhenitsyn after the collapse of the Soviet Union. Solzhenitsyn, too, sought to regenerate Russia by reconnecting her to her Orthodox and pre-revolutionary past. In Russia's case, however, it was a fruitless endeavour because, after seventy years of totalitarianism and the physical extinction of all the old elites and their descendants, there was nothing left to revive. France had been more fortunate. The fires of the past had been damped down but never extinguished. Of course the republican and the Catholic traditions were poles apart, but if the new idea of France was lofty enough, as de Gaulle insisted that it must be, then instead of the two traditions continuing to be antithetical they could begin, for the first time, to complement each other.

It was at this juncture, however, that de Gaulle, having indicated the way ahead, withdrew to Colombey les Deux Églises, leaving the Fourth Republic, under the parliamentary system, to prove its worth or, as some would say, to give it enough rope to hang itself. To begin with all went well. Post-war reconstruction got off to a flying start and the parliamentarians proved well capable of dealing with quasi-insurrectional industrial troubles fomented largely by the Communist party. What brought the Fourth Republic down, however, was potentially violent resistance to the Paris government's decision to grant independence to Algeria by ultra-royalists and Catholic generals, backed by the *pieds noirs* (the French settlers) – the last flick of that old dragon's tail, so to speak. So in 1958 de Gaulle, his most historic moment having arrived, returned triumphantly to Paris to set up the Fifth Republic under a constitution of his own devising: government by parties was replaced by presidential rule. To all intents and purposes, President de Gaulle became King – a veritable reincarnation of Louis XIV. Also in the making was a bureaucracy fit for this reincarnation of the Sun King. For by now, after ten years in operation, products of the ENA – the *énarques* – included in its ranks as many high-flyers steeped in the Catholic-monarchical tradition as those imbued with the revolutionary republican tradition. It was a significant innovation because one of the recurrent complaints about the French bureaucracy under the Third Republic had been that it was 'an automatic embodiment of Reason that was foreign to the soul and to the eternal mission of France' – a bureaucracy *sitting* on French soil rather than one *planted* in that soil. The ENA had put an end to that lament, as well as the soul unmistakably back into the machine.

Here is how Pierre Birnbaum describes the *énarques* in *The Idea of France*:

Probity, virtue and a belief that they had been called to public service interposed themselves against all forms of clientism and corruption. A sense of the grandeur of the state and of the privileges of public power, guaranteed that policy would be concerned chiefly with questions of equity. High level civil servants saw themselves as incarnating the power of the state – an active, controlling state, and one that was all the more legitimate because it held itself aloof from politics, from parties, ideologies and electoral strategies founded on compromise and client relationships that were harmful to the public interest. The most surprising thing about many of these high ranking servants of the state is the strength of their Catholic convictions. Like General de Gaulle himself, many described themselves as practising – in some cases very devout – Catholics, attending mass every Sunday in the fashionable districts of Paris, going on retreat at various abbeys and so on . . . In a striking turn of events, then, the state now drew its most devoted servants from the ranks of those who formerly were the declared enemies of the Republic . . . Removed from the world of politics and business, with their compromises of principle and reckless risk taking, and protected against the temptations of money, these high ranking bureaucrats – often heirs to a family tradition of public service – displayed their loyalty to the state at every opportunity.

To describe such a body as a bureaucracy – that is, officials paid by the State – is to give a rather misleading impression, not only in the sense that many of its more successful functionaries were replacing the elected deputies – mostly lawyers, teachers, doctors and journalists – as governmental ministers, but also in the sense that they themselves conceived their role quite as much to rule as to administer. Just as de Gaulle was rather more a king than a president, so in all but name were the *énarques* as much humanistic and aristocratic as legalistic and bureaucratic; and increasingly hereditary too, since dynasties began to form. Drawn over-whelmingly from the ranks of the haute bourgeoisie, genera-tion after generation of *énarques* succeeded each other at the highest level, forming in the process an interlocking network of highly educated and cultured families sharing a common tradition of dedication to the public weal. In theory, of course, it was a meritocracy – a career open to all ranks of society – but in practice entry was controlled by tests of quality and character far transcending anything that could be discovered through competitive examinations alone: tests of character and quality set and judged by the haute bourgeoisie itself. Soon it had become the highest calling in the land, conferring greater social status than that achieved by merely winning elections. But unlike the pre-vious science-based Third Republic bureaucracy, which had been largely made up of anti-religious or atheistic utilitarians with economic efficiency as their organizing principle, this Fifth Republic replacement included more than its fair share of practising Catholics, most of whom had come under the influence of the great Catholic theologian of the period, Jacques Maritain, not to mention Montaigne, whose famous essays had done so much to redefine France's ethics of nobil-ity in a Christian rather than a stoic Roman mode; in favour, that is, of clemency and mercy over revenge and cruelty, and of persuasion over force. In fact the ENA was a bureaucracy not so much of experts and technicians governing by a rule book as of statesmen governing by a code of ethics; as such it was very much more immune than most to the iron law condemning bureaucracy to end up putting the interests of their own organization before those of the nation.

Thus it was that President Charles de Gaulle, a reincarnation of the Sun King, who had rendered France's *ancien-régime* aristocracy dysfunctional in the seventeenth century, perfected, in the 1960s, what became to all intents and purposes a new well-functioning aristocracy. And it functioned, for a decade, to great effect. Through the invention of indicative planning – a system that combined the free market with a large measure of governmental guidance – France's economy was effectively modernized. Even more impressive, the *énarques* were triumphantly successful in shaping the institutions of the new European community in such a way as to best serve the interests of France. This was done, of course, in the early days before Britain had become a member of the club – and while the German official class was still completely *hors de combat* – but it says a lot about the *énarques'* far-sighted sagacity that while the British political class was concentrating all its energies and imagination on transforming old imperial territories in Asia and Africa into a new and almost completely worthless Commonwealth, their French contemporaries had stolen a march by creating a new French empire on the European continent. Moreover it was also at this period that the *énarques*, taking a look at the future, saw the wisdom of maintaining a distance from the USA – a distance, too, from any absolute faith in the global economy that was already in the process of taking shape. Such clarity of vision – and, equally important, the necessary will to follow a settled course in line with that vision – could never

183

have materialized out of the rough-and-tumble of parliamentary politics, nor indeed out of an open, classless elite drawn from all the different sections of society. The necessary unity and cohesion could only come out of a relatively small group who shared not only the same organizational values at work but also the same personal and family values – in short, a social as well as a professional elite. In terms of foreign policy and military affairs, the need for such a small governing 'ascendancy' – unaccountable and untransparent and therefore able to act decisively and quickly – has always been seen as a necessary part, in practice if not in theory, of a well-ordered democracy. Gaullist France, however, was the first to see that in the interconnected world of the future, such an essentially aristocratic group, with the confidence to act decisively, would have a crucial part to play on many other fronts as well – notably in matters to do with world trade. Another point, particularly applicable to France, is also worth mentioning. Only an official class with the extra cachet that comes from exclusivity would have enough confidence not to be overawed by France's notoriously arrogant circle of world-famous Paris intellectuals dominated at the time by Jean-Paul Sartre.

But there was still more to it than that. For the socially exclusive *énarchie* possessed another quality that made it indispensable: its ability – which parliamentary government in France notoriously lacked – to attract France's best and brightest away from the better-remunerated fields of private business and the media into politics. Once again the French official class was ahead of the game. For as early as 1960 they recognized that a democratic state would eventually have to find a way of competing with free-market forces in the all-important business of attracting into its service quality talent. The ENA was the answer. For not only did it enable its graduates to become government ministers, it also enabled them to head the various state enterprises and even, eventually, to take top jobs, on temporary loan, to private corporations, thereby ensuring that in France at least an element of the public-service ethic reached into parts where, in other countries, it was draining away.

De Gaulle himself, of course, was dethroned after the student *événements* of 1968[*] – that decade's most puerile and mindless act of destruction. But the ENA and the *énarques* escaped unscathed. Their setbacks, which had more to do with the arrogance that proverbially goes with great power, did not start until two decades later. Corruption set in and a series of scandals, beginning with the infamous contamination of blood supplies to hospitals. Unlike in the past, however, when such scandals only involved parliamentary politicians, these involved the *énarques* themselves – by then France's equivalent to the English Establishment. Parliamentarians of all parties were quick to take revenge by calling for the ENA to be abolished or, a worse fate, to be banished from Paris to the provinces – or, worst of all,

---

[*] What happened was De Gaulle lost the referendum in 1969 proposing constitutional changes – regional government and a weakening of the Senate. Many feared that the latter proposal was designed to curb an independent check on the regimes; and, for the first time in the Fifth Republic, an alternative non-threatening leader was available in Pompidou, who had been sacked by the General after dealing successfully with the 1968 student revolt.

turned into the equivalent of the Harvard Business School. Naturally enough, de Gaulle's presidential successors, Mitterrand and then Chirac, pretended to bend to these popular and populist whims, happy to promise reforms which would make the ENA more open, more answerable to the people, less remote, less impersonal, more human, more acceptable: in a word, less aristocratic. But nothing changed for long. From time to time the ranks of the *énarques* were thinned out but they soon filled up again; and although as the twentieth century drew to a close there was more and more talk of decentralization and the importance of civil society, in reality the rule of the *énarques* continued, chastened but unbowed, as much under governments of the Left as of the Centre and Right. If a few Old Etonians still seem to crop up in all British administrations, this is absolutely nothing to the number of *énarques* who appear at the top of every French administration. In spite of this brazen inequality – perhaps because of it – the system works, and in spite of its so-called bureaucratic despotism, the people don't hesitate to take to the streets, with impunity, if the *énarques* get unacceptably out of touch. As for the *hauteur* of the official class, few seem to mind. Rather the opposite, as they seem to like the idea of dignified leaders who look the part, speak the part, dress the part, and do not make much, or any, effort to pretend to be like everybody else. Indeed the French people, whose will not to be drawn like a flock of sheep has been so often demonstrated in the past, seem to welcome leaders who keep their distance, taking this as a sign not so much of disrespect for the masses as of self-respect and self-control, and recognizing, perhaps, that an ability to maintain 'an inner distance' within a democratic world is a valuable test of authenticity. In any case, what does it say of the dignity of a great nation that is prepared to tolerate being governed by ill-bred parvenus?[*]

In this respect France is indeed exceptional. For example, in an article in *Le Figaro* in 1999.[†] M. Secret, president of the union of administrators and inspectors general, after eating very humble pie about a string of new ENA scandals, ignores all the proposals for remedial and constitutional reform, preferring instead, in almost so many words, to call eloquently for a restoration of moral purpose, not to say *noblesse oblige*. The tone took me back to that of a public-school headmaster in the 1930s calling on the boys to live up to the time-honoured code of the English gentleman. Only in France, however, could this *de haut en bas* language still be acceptable. And the reason for this, I believe, is that only in France has there evolved, in the last half of the twentieth century, due to the blessed reconnection of *La France moderne* with *La France profonde*, a concept of superiority that owes as much to Montaigne as to Robespierre: a concept, therefore, as acceptable to the snobberies of the Right as to those of the Left.

In Britain, however, we are moving very perilously in the

---

[*] Max Weber, *Political Writings*, ed. Peter Lassman and Ronald Speirs, Cambridge Texts in the History of Political Thought (Cambridge: Cambridge University Press, 1994).
[†] Quoted in Larry Siedentop's *Democracy in Europe* published by Allen Lane (Penguin, 2000).

opposite direction. Just as the French revolutionaries two hundred years ago were determined to eliminate all traces of Gallic Catholicism, France's national religion, because of its association with France's *ancien régime*, so now Britain's current modernizing radicals of both the Left and the Right are determined to eliminate Britain's national religion because of its association with our *ancien régime*. By national religion I do not mean religion in the deepest sense of that which puts men in touch with the divine. That, as far as it exists, is still Christianity. I mean rather a national religion in the more down-to-earth, non-doctrinal sense of an ethical and moral system in accordance with which people try to lead their lives; and that, I submit, until very recently, was the code of the English gentleman. When, in the nineteenth century, faith in Christianity weakened, the sub-Christian cult of the English gentleman enormously increased its hold, and during my lifetime became the main moral force holding the nation together and determining the manner and manners in which individuals and classes treated each other. It is this moral force, along with the institutions that supported it, that both consciously and unconsciously, for reasons of misplaced idealism or cynical political opportunism, the radical modernizers on both the Right and the Left are very successfully seeking to destroy.

Nowadays anyone who mentions the word 'gentleman' can expect to receive a mocking response, rather as I imagine anyone who might mention the word 'comrade' would do in contemporary Russia. Whereas once any Englishman would be proud to be called a gentleman, today he would fear it might render him unemployable. Arguably this represents progress. I will consider this possibility in a moment. But what has to be done first is to consider the downside, the price being paid for this progress, if it is progress. It has meant, as I say, the destruction of one element, in my view the most important element, of Britain's moral order. An immense unravelling has taken place. And for the time being no one knows how they are meant to behave. The old moral compass has been disconnected and nothing has yet been put in its place. For me and most of my friends and contemporaries – and to a lesser extent for most of my children's generation – the code of the English gentleman, far more than the Ten Commandments, was what kept us up to the moral mark; and it was fear of being caught out in ungentlemanly behaviour that acted as a far more effective deterrent to bad behaviour than fear of hellfire. All classes were affected in this way, not – as was once the case – only those who were born into the social status of a gentleman, or those who aspired to that status; it also affected those who, while in no way imagining that they themselves would become part of the elect, found a great deal to admire and emulate in those who were. For that is the crucial development in the concept of the English gentleman that took place in the nineteenth century: its transformation from a high rank in a social hierarchy to an ideal that caught the imagination, entertained, and even impressed all ranks in that hierarchy. Gentlemanliness was such a loose concept that it seeped into everything, providing models as much for sportsmanship as for statesmanship; as much for business and banking as for the Civil Service; as much for the world of scholarship as for the world of the dilettante; and for both public and private life. Gentlemanliness was a universal presence, like that of the Almighty. Only a very few of the grandest of aristocrats – to whom the restraints of gentlemanliness, they thought, could not possibly apply – and the very poorest of the poor – who, for different reasons felt likewise – dared cock a snook.

I don't think I am exaggerating. The moral hold of the ideals of the English gentleman was one of the wonders of the modern world. There was nothing like it in the rest of Europe. It determined the relationship between lawyers and clients, doctors and patients, employers and employees, military officers and privates, MPs and constituents, givers and receivers, governors and governed, and even parsons and parishioners. Into all these relationships, and many more, it introduced an extra sensitivity and finesse lacking in the same relationships elsewhere.* Having myself been accustomed to an England where these relationships still obtained, I am almost constantly shocked by their absence today, by the great tycoon whose corporation has laid off thousands of the workforce who finds nothing disgraceful, on that very same day, about accepting a pay rise for himself of, say, half a million pounds; or the journalist who publishes

---

* That is why, in old England, the Napoleonic idea of 'a career open to all the talents' never quite applied. For in Britain, ideally, something else over and above was required: a willingness to play, or at any rate to pretend to play, by certain historic rules: rules with roots sunk deep into the feudal past.

190

in his paper information gained over lunch which ruins a Cabinet Minister's career; or an officer and gentleman who tries to raise money by selling his mistress's love letters; most of all, by the recent evidence that such moral confusion is not one wit less prevalent in the corridors of power than it is in every other walk of life. Of course such misdeeds have always occurred. But what is new is that those who behave in this way seem to have no shame and go about their dirty business blithely unaware of having dirt on their hands. It is the same in small matters: the young man who puts up his dirty boots on the opposite railway carriage seat or who uses foul language in the hearing of an old lady, etc., etc., etc. There is no point in rebuking such people, for they know not what they do. It is almost as if the English people, once proud to be a nation of gentlemen, suddenly feel a pressing need to show, at every possible opportunity and in every possible way, as much as at the top of society as at the bottom, that they have become instead a nation of non-gentlemen, if not of anti-gentlemen.

Today, in my experience, there is only one group of English people who still use the word gentleman in a friendly sense, and they are those incorrigibly dyed-in-the-wool reactionaries, London cab-drivers, one of whom was heard, not so long ago – after having had Tony Benn as a passenger – commenting thus: 'I hate his views, squire, but I would say this of him, he was a true gent.'* For the rest,

---

* See Philip Mason, *The English Gentleman* (London: André Deutsch, 1982).

however, gentlemanliness, once synonymous with selflessness and dutifulness, with concern for others, indeed with
Englishness itself, has become, if not a dirty word, then a
word likely to elicit at best a sneer or a snigger and at worst
even a snarl.

The reasons, of course, are well known. The pattern of
behaviour for a gentleman was rooted in *ancien régime* inequality. It was the beautiful flower that grew out of a soil
well manured with privilege. It was a manner and a style
the upper classes had adopted to charm the lower classes
into deference, into touching their caps. All these are fair
complaints. Gentlemanliness had indeed grown out of a
hierarchic social order, with which it was inextricably connected. Moreover, in the years following the French Revolution, when Britain's upper classes were fearful for their
heads, it had been used by them to exclude and humiliate
the middle classes and by the middle classes to exclude and
humiliate the working classes. That relaxed fluidity in social
relations that had characterized the eighteenth century had,
under the influence of fear, begun to harden. Barriers had
become less easy to climb over or under. So there were
reasons, if you were looking for them – as radicals always are
– to see the idea of the English gentleman as a force for reaction, just as there had been even better reasons for the French
revolutionaries to see Catholicism in an even worse light.

Nevertheless, interestingly enough, when the socialists
swept into power in 1945 they didn't feel this resentment
against Old Britain in general and the gentleman in particular. Rather the opposite. Under socialists, Old Britain

and New Britain seemed to make common cause. Just as Gaullism had the effect of bringing the two halves of France together, so socialism had something of the same effect on post-war Britain. This was not at all what was expected to happen. Old Britain feared the worst. Serving in the army in Holland on the morning after the news of Labour's land-slide victory reached us, I noticed a significant change in the ablution rituals of a very grand fellow-officer in the Grenadier Guards in the next-door tent. In the previous months of campaigning, through thick and thin, his officer-servant had every morning laid out for his lordship's use a coroneted ivory set of hairbrushes, a coroneted silver shaving bowl and water jug, and a coroneted white linen towel. On this particular morning, however, Lord X ordered these emblems of nobility to be replaced by a set of plebeian general service utensils for the use of other ranks. Assuming that the tumbrels were about to roll, he had decided that discretion was the better part of valour. Nor was he alone in withdrawing his head from above the parapet. That same morning the squadron's lines of communication back to England were jammed with rich officers instructing their stockbrokers to sell or buy, or do whatever seems best when the end of the world is nigh, or rather Nye.*

In the event, however, this panic was unnecessary. The old order was never in any serious danger. Some indication that this might be so was vouchsafed to me by my admirably

---

* Nye was the nickname of Aneurin Bevan, the left-wing firebrand who later described all Tories as 'lower than vermin'.

detached step-uncle, Ronnie Norman (Montagu Norman's younger brother), whom I visited on leave later that summer. For the advent of a socialist government with an overwhelming majority had not troubled his serenity one little bit. 'Don't worry too much about English socialism,' he said. 'It will be run along the same gentlemanly, amateur and inefficient lines as English capitalism has been run.'

Gentlemanliness, he insisted, had put its stamp on all classes – not just on the upper class but on the middle and lower classes as well. This was one of Britain's unique achievements: to have developed an ideal of superior behaviour that could be democratized. So, just as gentlemanliness had civilized first the aristocracy and then the bourgeoisie, so it would now do the same for the proletariat. This could not have happened in Germany, he surmised. The ethical code of the German Junker or the German professor was totally untransferable. So was the Japanese ideal of the scholar-mandarin. But Britain was different, which was why it had been such nonsense, my uncle went on, for Churchill to make an election broadcast trying to frighten the voters by arguing that socialism must lead to rule by the Gestapo.*

I know one won't find much evidence of this form of sanity in the conservative newspapers of the time, or in the speeches from the Tory back benches of the House of Commons, or even in private correspondences. But such an

---

* Churchill got this idea from a bestseller of the period by Professor F. A. Hayek called *The Road to Serfdom*.

absence is to be expected, since *grands rentiers* like Ronnie Norman did not 'air their views' to all and sundry; were indeed very private persons, their passion for privacy being the source of their dignity and authority. But their public silence should not be taken to denote a lack of private influence. To a degree the historians will never do justice to, the best of Old England always felt *quietly* confident of its continued place under English socialism, and in the event this confidence turned out to be justified.

For change under the Attlee government was indeed channelled and managed in such a gentlemanly way that the organic growth of the established institution of State and society – monarchy, the Church and the social hierarchy, property and the family – were not fundamentally threatened. Nor was there any fundamental or irreversible distribution of property. As for the creation of the welfare state – an experiment started a century earlier by Bismarck in Prussia – that was something many Conservatives were inclined in private to approve of – on paternalistic grounds. The argument, so powerfully championed in recent years by Correlli Barnett, that the Labour government should have been concentrating instead on using Marshall Aid to rebuild Britain's economic infrastructure, would have cut no ice with my Uncle Ronnie. He thought that the welfare state was the appropriate reward to the returning soldiers and their families.* In the

---

* At a later date he used the same argument to justify allowing coloured immigrants into Britain. 'If they were good enough to fight and die for Britain, they are good enough to live in Britain.'

same spirit he did not object to the increased clout of the trade unions in industrial relations. The workers deserved a better deal. As for punitive taxation of the rich, that too could be justified as a necessary economic price to pay in return for Labour's willingness to leave the social hierarchy, and the political and educational institutions that sustained it, unscathed. It was a statesmanlike compromise. England's officer and gentlemen class, in return for being allowed to continue running the show – literally so, since there were as many grandees occupying the 'commanding heights' of the nationalized industries as there had been on those of the private industries – agreed to run the show in a more generous spirit. The free-enterprise, hardline, capitalist side of the Conservative Party disliked this compromise. But in those days it was not the free-enterprise hardliners who ran the party, any more than it was the socialist hardliners who ran the Labour Party. So gentlemanliness prevailed. The two great parties abided by the gentlemanly rules. From the Conservatives came an agreement to help make the welfare state work and to make capitalism more acceptable to the workers; from the Labour side there was agreement to let a chastened upper class carry on much as before. Old Etonians and their like, for example, were not reduced to being 'superfluous men', as their French equivalents had been during the Third Republic. They went on being taught to regard the governance of England as their personal responsibility, and to believe that if they did not set an example of civilized standards of behaviour, then the country would go to pot. Nor is this just the case of chickens running around after their heads have been chopped off. For a planned socialist economy had a genuine and desperate need for the services of men and women with the ethics of public service bred into the marrow of their bones to be put in charge of the commanding heights. Although equality of opportunity, on the American model, might produce the best entrepreneurs, something very different was required to produce socialist public servants – something bound to be very similar to the patrician-producing social system already in existence. So instead of destroying the system, how much more sensible to adapt it to socialist purposes. Instead of pulling up the feudal roots, graft socialist ideas onto them; and do so with a clear socialist conscience because there was an inimitable moral quality about British inequality that accorded rather better with socialism than it did with capitalism. Thus it was that Eton and the public schools, and indeed the whole structure dedicated to producing a gentlemanly governing class, did not become an irrelevant anachronism fit only for the historical dustbin. It became instead the only *ancien régime* with at least a relatively assured fate.

I remember very clearly, for example, a social gathering at More Place – Ronnie Norman's Hertfordshire country house – at which there were several doctors from the local cottage hospital, of which he was chairman. It must have been about 1946 and they were all up in arms against Aneurin Bevan's plan to set up a National Health Service. Norman's view, however, was that in the climate of the time such a battle could not be won. There was no way the doctors could fight such a battle without giving the impression that they were putting their selfish financial interests before the interests of the patients. Not only were they bound to lose the battle, but in the process the high reputation of the medical profession as a whole would be damaged. What Norman was doing, in effect, was to urge the doctors to live up to gentlemanly standards of distinguished conduct. Whether, in the event, those particular doctors took the hint I do not know. But what I do remember is the effect his words had upon the level of discourse that followed. It was raised and broadened immeasurably. None of the doctors present wanted to let the side down. At that period the whole nation was conscious of the existence of this obligation, and if they were inclined to forget it there were enough Ronnie Normans around to remind them where their duty lay. Here was a form of influence at work that transcended party politics. At the same period the parliamentary Conservative Party was busy stirring up the doctors to fight to the last ditch. That was what the Conservative grass roots seemed to want. But in those days there still existed a small number of influential private individuals spread across the land, with the benefit of a stable tradition and wide social horizons, and enough wealth and property to ensure their independence, who could and did offer a quality of leadership superior to anything to be expected from politicians with their ears, by necessity, glued to the ground.

But as the case of the doctors shows, this gentlemanly ideal of distinguished conduct, upheld so quietly but formidably by Ronnie Norman and his ilk, was not by any means always in line with the principles of a market economy. Indeed quite often it was distinctly out of line. A mixed economy, paternalist but not dirigiste, suited the gentlemanly ideal of distinguished conduct best; made it possible, that is, for the best of Old Britain and the best of New Britain to put their joint shoulders to the wheel. Gentlemanly socialism may sound a contradiction in terms. But that, under Major Attlee, was what it amounted to – a pinkish, as against a bluish, variety of paternalism. So the separation of Old Britain from New Britain, which was expected to happen under socialism after the war, only really began to happen when the collapse of communism in the Soviet Union, and the final laying of the communist ghost, allowed for the triumphant emergence of global capitalism. For triumphant capitalism, unlike triumphant socialism after the war, had no need to make use of the gentlemanly public-service ethics. Quite the contrary. It had a vested interest in the destruction of that ethic, and the marginalization of the gentlemanly class that still adhered to it. Cutting off heads, in the French revolutionary fashion, was not necessary. A less brutal but no less effective method was to stuff their mouths with gold. Whereas socialism had taken the high road into the heart of the gentry by appealing to their sense of public duty, capitalism took the low road by tempting them into private gain: *Forget all that old-fashioned* noblesse oblige *claptrap and get your snouts into the trough with the rest of us.* To many of the great landed aristocratic families the appeal was irresistible. Here was an utterly unexpected turn-up for the book; a miraculous opportunity to repair the family houses and fortunes. What is more, there could now be safety in numbers, since instead of being an endangered species – as the great landed aristocrats had become resigned to believing themselves to be – they now had a chance of becoming just another indistinguishable, and therefore safe, billionaire, occupying a relatively humble rank in the new international plutocracy. It was an offer difficult to refuse. Just as much of the old order had risen to the challenge of making socialism work – by being true to the public service ethic – so did much of the old order rise to the challenge of making capitalism work, by being false to the public service ethic. Unsurprisingly, it was not long before the institutions that had helped over the generations to produce the old upper class – the public schools and Oxbridge – adjusted to this new state of affairs. Instead of continuing to inculcate the public-service ethic, they started to inculcate the spirit of free enterprise. Instead of teaching their pupils culture so that they might become connoisseurs, they taught them culture so that they might get jobs as adults at Christie's and Sotheby's selling off the artistic treasures generations of ancestors had spent their lives collecting. Success – it was called 'achievement' – became the name of the game, to the point where a great public school like Eton became just as proud of an old alumni who had built up a media empire from scratch as of one who had become a prime minister or an archbishop.*

Superficially, of course, this has all left the old order seemingly in place. In a recent book Andrew Adonis has a whole section arguing that the English aristocracy in particular and the old order in general are now in a stronger position than they have ever been before. Hereditary peers, he points out, still have a political base in the House of Lords, which, because of the innovation of Life Peers, seems even more indestructible today than at any moment since the death of Queen Victoria. As for Eton and the other public schools, they still produce a vastly unfair number of generals, judges, and MPs. Most striking of all, the great landed families have never had it so good since the heyday of the Edwardian era.† All this is true. In material terms much has been left unchanged. But deep down, because the public-service ethic has gone, everything has changed because it was this ethic that justified the unfairness, that gave the whole show its life and purpose. Eton illustrates this point to sad perfection. For unlike in the United States,

---

* Of all the old Etonians in the House of Commons today, only Oliver Letwin carries any authority, and what makes him so distinctive, so head and shoulders above his contemporaries, so effortlessly superior, is not what he learnt at school but what he learnt from his beautiful American academic mother, Shirley Letwin, rightly famous as the author of that most enthusiastic and eloquent celebration of the English gentleman, her classic work *The Gentleman in Trollope: Individuality and Moral Conduct* (1982).

† In this connection I read in a newspaper gossip column recently that the grandson of my wartime brother officer had just celebrated his return to the ancient family pile, dispensing enough caviar to give all eight hundred guests their fill.

where inequality has always been justified as the reverse side of the freedom coin, here it has always been seen as the necessary price to be paid for a high-quality governing class, on the principle that while plutocrats and meritocrats can be produced in one generation, it takes several generations of privilege to produce gentlemen dedicated to the public service. To do that, therefore, a society needs a social space at the top where advantage has reinforced itself across the generation. But under capitalism – where the public-service ethic is judged to be more a liability than an asset – that justification falls to the ground, rendering its precious product, the English gentleman, vulnerable to the charge of being unfaithful to the spirit of free enterprise, just as the French Revolution put the old Catholic order under suspicion of being unfaithful to the age of Enlightenment.

It is not only the triumph of capitalism, however, that has created a climate inimical to the gentlemanly ideal of public service; so, to an even more dangerous degree, has the latest intellectual fashion of anathematizing the past, of which the gentlemanly code of dignified behaviour is such an integral part – quite as much as Catholicism was of France's past. Inevitably, therefore, any programme of modernization in Britain is bound to rub out the gentlemanly stamp wherever it can be found, which is pretty well everywhere. Socialism, as has already been noted, never turned against the past *tout court*, only against the capitalist system. The new reforming intelligentsia are much more radical. They are bent on eradicating the past in its entirety. As Jonathan Clark has recently put it: 'Lifelong reformers who have at last accepted the market compound that sin by blaspheming against the ancestral Gods. For them, History did not deliver Utopia and History is therefore to be abolished.'*

The implications of this change are profound. For whereas the assumption used to be that the past is a source of strength – the source from which a nation draws its enduring characteristics – the new assumption is that the past, for the same reason, is a source of weakness. No effort must be spared, therefore, to abolish the national memory. Instead of something to be kept fresh, because it is the only way the nation has of knowing itself, it becomes something that must be erased, which is the best way for the nation to stop knowing itself. So, naturally, the new reforming initiatives tend to focus particularly on erasing symbols, institutions, and, above all, religious beliefs, since it is those, above all else, that keep the national memory alive. Only by inducing national amnesia through the eradication of all remnants of the *ancien régime* can a new nation come into being. Thus the whole idea of reform is transformed. Reformers used to envisage improving on the past, building on the past. Now they envisage forgetting the past. Today's intelligentsia, therefore, do not turn away from the past with indifference: they reach back into it to silence its message, and to silence those whose presence is bound to proclaim that message, than whom there is no more guilty party

---

* Jonathan Clark, *Our Shadowed Present: Modernism, Postmodernism and History* (Atlantic Books, 2003), 190.

than the English gentleman. In Jonathan Clark's phrase, the new intelligentsia's new idea is 'to privilege the present', which means in practice privileging the victims of the past – ethnic minorities, women, homosexuals, youth, and non-gentlemen – while deprivileging the beneficiaries of the past – whites, males, heterosexuals, the old, and, above all, gentlemen. By the same token it means deprivileging all the old moral standards and traditions, particularly those to do with public service (duty, decency, honesty, loyalty, faithfulness), and privileging instead a wholly new set with only one overriding principle: that of being the opposite of the old set of mores, customs, and traditions. Paradoxically, however, this determination to blank out the past has had the effect of blanking out the future also, because without a knowledge of the old it becomes impossible to plan for the new. So the grand schemes of social reform, previously framed by liberals and socialists, each with a clear historical genealogy and a specific picture of a better society, are rendered quite as irrelevantly anachronistic by this new way of thinking as the old conservatives' symbols and institutions. For they too are part of the tyranny of the past. The single most important thing is to start completely afresh, and since planning for the future cannot be done without reference to the past, it is best not to plan for the future.

'Presentism', as Jonathan Clark has christened it, might seem too absurd to worry about. How can it be possible to consign history so thoroughly to the dustbin? Unfortunately presentism has an attractively simple solution. Not only does it seek to anathematize the past but also to trivialize it. It urges us not to believe in roots; not to think of the customs, mores, traditions, and beliefs of the past as deeply rooted. They are, the presentists insist, relatively modern inventions, and as easily as they were invented, they can be disinvented and reinvented again. Presentism does not believe in roots. It believes roots are what ruling classes invent to make radical change seem much more difficult than it need be. Most traditions, presentists argue, were invented and they can be reinvented just as easily. This is even true, they suggest, of Britain's sense of national identity. It, too, is a recent fabrication. Instead of seeing the nation state as a great oak with deep roots, the presentists portray it as something more like a potted plant. Because Old Britain was designed in the eighteenth century by one group of beneficiaries to suit themselves, so the aggrieved victims of that earlier construct can now design a New Britain to their own liking. Having been done many times before, it can be done again.

Characteristic of this new radicalism is the devaluation of the word 'revolution'. Unlike the French revolutionaries, who were acutely conscious of the historic nature of their great undertaking and of the enormity of the risks it involved – to be compared in gravity with a heart-transplant operation on the body politic – these new English radicals envisage the replacement of Old Britain with New Britain as being something more in the order of exchanging last year's out-of-date model of a car for this year's up-to-date one. In other words, presentism takes the sting out of change. Whereas radicalism was formerly a frightening concept, seeming to call in question all sorts of precious things like stability and property, now it can be seen to be threatening only things that are already out of date, decrepit, decaying, on their last legs, as good as dead. Here, in a marriage made in heaven or hell – according to your point of view – the new forces of presentism merge happily with the new forms of capitalist triumphalism, the latter being as cavalier in its attitudes to the past and the reality of roots as the former. Indeed presentism could be said to fit capitalism like a glove. For capitalism, too, warms to the idea of a world in constant change and renewal. It, too, is no respecter of customs and traditions. What is more, capitalism feels a natural sympathy with presentism because as well as having no time for old-fashioned conservatism and tradition, presentism has no time for old-fashioned socialism and liberal reform either.

A good example of these two forces working together is to be found in what is currently threatening Oxbridge. Presentists hate Oxbridge because it is old and the free-enterprise culture hates Oxbridge because it has concentrated in the past on producing gentlemanly public servants rather than go-getting entrepreneurs. So how can both these hates be sated? The answer is by the State forcing Oxbridge to start concentrating on the production of entrepreneurs rather than public servants. Whereas Oxbridge's proudest boast in the past was to be able, in four or five years, to transform socially ambitious and clever working-class lads, like John Buchan, into a passable imitation of old Etonians, in the future it will have to boast of being able, in the same period of time, to turn old Etonians into passable imitations of thrustingly ambitious working-class lads. The difficulty here, of course, is that Oxbridge colleges grew out of a long tradition of educating well-heeled young men who could expect to lead lives of relative dignity and leisure. So unless the colleges change their ways out of all recognition, they will be very bad at producing ambitious young meritocrats well equipped to win the rat race. But even if they do manage to adapt to this purpose, and successfully start educating the country's most promising runners in the rat race, is that likely to be any less unfair to those excluded than the present system? One can see that it is a system of exclusion that may suit the needs of the market more satisfactorily than the old system, but is that to be judged synonymous with serving the cause of equality of opportunity? Not by any means, I would have thought. Gentlemanliness, as we have seen, was something that all classes could aspire to, and in some ways it put fewer hurdles in the way of the underprivileged in getting to Oxbridge than does the present need to demonstrate, at an early age, a thrusting ambition to make money.

In this respect, too, it is worth considering the case of my old newspaper, *The Times*. The culture in the pre-Murdoch days used to be very much like that of an Oxbridge college: dignified and leisurely, without great pressure for scoops or intellectual sensationalism. In fact the pressure was all the other way. Gentlemanliness was the order of the day. The leader writers, of whom I was a junior one, were served tea – toasted teacakes and strawberry jam, etc. – by uniformed parlour maids in what had once been the proprietor's private house. One of my colleagues had been to Eton, but the rest had made it to Oxbridge from grammar schools. Their devotion to gentlemanly values, however, was nonetheless absolute. None of this type survived the takeover by Rupert Murdoch, except one old Etonian, Charles Douglas-Home, who showed himself remarkably well equipped to win the rat race. But is *The Times* a better newspaper? Unquestionably it is more open to the recruitment of one type of journalist than it used to be, but I would not fancy the chances of any applicant – either from a state or from a public school – who insisted that there was such a thing as public-service journalism. All systems are unfair in their different ways, and if Old Britain was unfair to those who spoke common, the new system is unfair to those who refuse to act common.

It would seem to me, therefore, that the current Left–Right consensus in favour of a classless society is a bit of a con trick. The distinguished historian David Cannadine, in his book *Class in Britain* (1998), as much acclaimed on the Left as on the Right, spelt out what it would involve. 'In order to render the hierarchical model of class inapplicable', he writes, 'the visible manifestations of hierarchy would have to go. This would mean doing more than abolishing the rights of hereditary peers to sit in the House of Lords. It would mean the blanket abolition of titles: not just life peers and knighthoods but also hereditary peers and baronetcies. The abolition of titles would, of course, go some way to abolishing the sense of upper-class separateness. The Duke of Westminster would still be a very rich man as the non-ducal Mr Grosvenor. But he would no longer be an aristocrat.'

What is it about aristocratic separateness that requires such symbolic annihilation? Clearly it is no longer the great economic and social power that used to come with wealth and land, since Mr Grosvenor, in a classless society, would still possess as much wealth and land as ever he did as Duke of Westminster; nor even the hereditary seat in the parliamentary upper house that the Duke of Westminster has already lost. Still less can it be the old objection – which was once valid – that by putting its own exclusive stamp on good taste in music and literature, on correct pronunciation, on high fashion, on good table manners, etc., the aristocrats had, in effect, excluded all other classes from sharing in these good things for their own sake, as against deferentially adopting them for the purposes of social climbing. Fifty years ago that objection certainly did hold water. But it has long ceased to do so. Today it is the lower rather than the upper classes who are being encouraged to put their stamp on all these good things. So in what way would taking away the Duke of Westminster's title to nobility and reducing him to the status of a billionaire commoner make him less separate? Only in one way that I can think of. It would symbolically lift from his shoulders the duties and obligations traditionally associated with that high rank. Let me illustrate what I mean.

Many years ago I had a small basement flat on the Westminster Estate, and when the Duke of Westminster's agent wrote in a very peremptory manner to inform me and my fellow tenants of His Grace's intention to put up our rents we wrote a joint letter begging him to think again. Its burden was that as tenants of a Duke we thought we had a right to expect more considerate treatment. While run-of-the-mill landlords might think it all right to jack up the rent in this way, surely an aristocratic landlord really ought to know better. In other words, we appealed to his sense of *noblesse oblige*. As far as I can remember, the letter did not win us many favours. But the fact that we hoped it might illustrates a point that needs making, which is that the only way in which aristocrats are separate today – separate, that is, from all the other very rich people – is that higher standards are expected of them. While today it comes as no surprise to find a business tycoon with his snout in the trough, it is still shocking to find a duke so engaged. By and large, aristocrats are no longer expected to be rich and powerful. But they are still expected to behave like gentlemen, and if the Duke of Westminster – come the classless society – really wants to show that, as Mr Grosvenor, he is no longer hatefully separate, no longer hatefully aristocratic, the best and surest way for him to do so will be, as his first act as a commoner landlord, to evict from his estate a lot of aged gentlefolk in reduced circumstances. Today, therefore, the sense of separateness, the removal of which is the major purpose of creating the classless society, arises no longer, as formerly, from exceptional privilege, but from exceptional obligation. Yes, the Duke of Westminster will be reduced to the status of being just one of a whole class of other super-rich Misters; but the reduction in status will have nothing to do with his material position in the world, which will not change at all, and everything to do with a change in his moral status, which will change subtly but significantly. So, in a miniscule way, will my status as a knight, and if in the classless society I am deprived of that title, the only difference will be the lifting of a small burden of moral obligation to give a rather larger tip than had been my wont before I was knighted.

So what would the symbolic ending of aristocratic separateness, and the ushering in of a classless society, really signify? Essentially it would signify the end of the tradition of *noblesse oblige*, the end of the tradition of linking power and wealth to the ideal of selflessness. What it won't signify to the slightest degree is any diminution of economic privilege or any closing of the gap between the rich and most of the poor. The rich have nothing to worry about, and the poor little to gain. Very much the opposite. For it will mark the moment when the rich fully inherit the kingdom because, with the disappearance of the aristocracy, the last ghostly remnant of a moral order laying obligations on the rich will have been symbolically excised from the national memory. What began as a reforming movement to abolish class consciousness is, therefore, in danger of ending up as a movement to abolish class *conscience*. Most of the vices of the class system having already been squeezed out by the old reformers, their successors have now been reduced to squeezing out the virtues. The worst example of the sheer *wrongness* of this classless 'project' can be found in the role it assigns to the monarchy. Let me once again refer to David

Cannadine's book, *Class in Britain*. He is vague on the monarchy, but putting my own gloss on his phrase that 'it may not be necessary to abolish it', and bearing in mind the new role he assigns to the Duke of Westminster, I would surmise that in a new classless Britain the Queen, renamed Mrs Windsor, will be left in possession of all her palaces and her wealth, but stripped of all her majesty; stripped, that is, of precisely that religious dimension that raises the spirits and wins the hearts of her people.

Down this path lies madness. It involves crossing the line that divides political radicalism from iconoclastic mania. Pressing on with attempts to turn Britain into a classless society is rather as if France today were to find it necessary to renew her old struggle to free her soil of Catholics and Catholicism, regardless of the fact that the old reasons for wanting to do so have entirely disappeared. Just as no one in his senses could suppose that France today suffers from an excess of clericalism, so no one in his senses could suppose that Britain suffers from an excess of aristocracy. Indeed it is not unusual to hear old Labour stalwarts saying that they are beginning to mourn the passing away of aristocracy. Better belted earls than Tony's cronies. This is enough, however, for when people begin to start missing something this means that they are beginning to remember why they loved it in the first place. Of course this does not mean they want the restoration of aristocracy, only that they recognize that the passing of aristocracy has left a gaping hole in the heart of Britain's body politic that middle-class meritocracy shows no signs of being able to fill. Which brings me back to the French comparison. France, too, as we have already seen, sought to slough off all traces of her *ancien régime* with dire consequences, and only returned to health again after making peace with her ancestral gods. A comparable spirit of reconciliation is required here. It is not a question of bringing the aristocracy back to life but rather of giving it a decent burial so that at least its spirit can live on.

Epilogue

Switzerland is Socialism in the sense in which that word expresses a principle hostile to the interests of true society – the elimination of superiorities.

Matthew Arnold

Privilete lay between us. But I had an intimation that it worked against him . . . His privilege – his house, his staff, his income, the acres he could look out at every day and knew to be his – this privilege could press him down into himself, into non-doing and nullity.

V. S. Naipaul on the landlord in his novel, *The Enigma of Arrival* (Viking, 1987)

Surprisingly, perhaps, I rather welcome the Labour government's decision to remove the last of the hereditary aristocrats from the House of Lords; at least I would do so if it were to mean that, as a result, the old political class as a whole were henceforth to be made to feel at home everywhere else. At the moment, of course, that is not the case, most particularly in the House of Commons. Constituency selection committees, for example, even true-blue ones, discriminate against applicants with any visible connection with aristocracy, unless they go to great lengths to disavow and disguise any compromisingly armigerous antecedents.

214

Hence the present Earl of Ancram's decision to be known as Mr Ancram. Far better to be plain Mr than Lord Snooty. As it happens, I feel the same as a mere non-hereditary knight. On visiting our local medical practice I never use the 'Sir' since it tends to muddle the staff and slow down rather than accelerate my progress to the head of the queue.

Of course there are still a very few quarters – Ascot has long given up the ghost – where grandee titles impress, but mostly they are now more a source of embarrassment than pride. Snobbery has been turned on its head. Instead of what used to be called the lower classes aspiring to the accents, clothes, manners and tastes of what used to be called the upper classes, the upper classes now aspire to the accents, clothes, manners and tastes of the lower classes.* Needless to say, there are still those in the media who bang on about the unfairness of the old class system, on how it saddles the working classes with a lifelong sense of inferiority and the upper classes with a life long sense of superiority. But this is yet another example of the media not living in the real world. In the real world the boot is on the other foot. The aristocracy has long since ceased to look down their noses. Far from lording it, it now is almost embarrassingly eager to eat humble pie.

Unfortunately, however, so long as the hereditary peers were still seen to be enjoying their privileges in the House of Lords, it was easy – all too easy – for class-conscious egalitarians to ignore or distort this new reality. The continued

---

* Instance: Tony Blair's adoption of an estuary accent.

existence of a State nobility with its privileges officially sanctioned by the constitution – something difficult, if not
impossible, to render compatible with democratic principles
– allowed these egalitarian enthusiasts to remain very much
in business – so much so, that they have succeeded in turning toffs, grandees, or anybody remotely recognizable as
a gentleman, into the only minority Britain's increasingly
inclusive society is now allowed to *exclude*. All races, all
colours, all religions and all sexual orientations – or almost
all – are welcome, but not the upper classes or any of the
traditions they stood for.

This is an absurd and highly damaging state of affairs. It
means that, because of their association with aristocracy,
anybody who has been to a public school or to Oxbridge
– which includes most of the judges, senior academics, Tory
MPs and many Labour MPs, most senior civil servants, and
most of the great and the good – is felt to be vaguely
sinister and suspect. While once such a provenance was an
advantage, guaranteeing a respectful hearing, today it is a
disadvantage, guaranteeing a hostile hearing. The effects are
dismaying. Instead of the best-educated and the best-
spoken citizens being able to take part in the public debate,
they are more likely than not, in deference to political correctness,* to keep their heads below the parapet. Even a
knowledge of the classics, for example, is now felt to be
something best not admitted lest it sends out aristocratic

---

* Consider the pathetically low quality of most television discussion
programmes.

vibes. The same is true of good taste and good manners. The most absurd recent example of this systematic devaluation of all those attributes that used to confer authority is the decision of the controller of BBC Two, Jane Root, to kill off the programme called 'Correspondent', because it had disturbing connotations with 'Eton-educated guys in white linen suits'.* So across the board there is now a bias against all forms of superiority. Thus the teacher must disguise his superior knowledge, the priest his superior holiness, the old their superior experience; and as for the master–pupil relationship, that is absolutely prohibited. Indeed pretty well every mark of charisma or authority is to be frowned upon as harking back to the reactionary customs of an aristocratic and hierarchical society. Even the relationship between donor and beneficiary has come under the same cloud since the giver is in danger of being accused of patrician patronage. To some extent, of course, these developments date back to the Enlightenment† and can be found in all Western societies; but they have been happening in Britain in the last quarter of the century with particular viciousness, not because Britain's hierarchical order was especially bad but because, being so successful, it was able to survive two hundred years longer than any other country's.

No one in their senses, surely, looking at Britain today, can possibly deny that the anti-aristocratic backlash, by de-legitimizing and rendering obsolete the very notion of

---

* See Anthony Howard, *The Times*, 9 December 2003.
† See Edward Skidelsky, *New Statesman*, 8 December 2003.

leadership – the word is now frowned upon not only in state schools but also in public schools – has already done more damage than any society can safely suffer without serious consequences. Yes, an hereditary nobility backed by constitutional privilege had to go. Yes, upper-class snobbery was an evil. Yes, Britain is better off without both. The curses of aristocracy have been removed. Unfortunately, however, so have many of the blessings. For in getting rid of Lord Snooty, whom Britain can well do without, we have also kicked out of play, so to speak, the values and traditions of the most various, stylish, eccentric, and above all fair-minded political class the Western world has ever known. This is too high a price to pay, and I would like to hope that the removal at long last of the hereditaries from the House of Lords might mark the moment when that fox was finally shot, thereby facilitating not only the reintegration of a valuable, if small, section of society back into our public life, but, much more importantly, the rehabilitation in our public life of the values, qualities, and traditions this section of society once stood for and embodied and which, for three centuries, guaranteed the rights and liberties of all the British people, so effectively as to make a written constitution unnecessary.

It is important to do so, I believe, because we are going through a period when a political class with these values and traditions is needed as never before. In theory, the old political class was pushed off into the wings to make room centre stage for the new democratically elected, open political class drawn from all sections of society. Sadly, however, it hasn't worked out like that. For what has replaced the old aristocratic political class is not a more open, meritocratic *political* class but a more open and meritocratic *economic* class: a class concerned more to make money than to make history, and more concerned with private than public affairs. The nation's commercial and financial sectors have been vastly opened up. Equality of opportunity has triumphed marvellously in those areas, to the great benefit of many individuals. But nobody can possibly say the effect has been anything but disastrous on Whitehall and Westminster, or, worst of all, on local government.

To some extent this was bound to happen, not just for the reasons already rehearsed in this essay – the need, for example, for 'new men' to feather their own individual and family nests before they can afford to bother about the national nest – but because, with the triumph of capitalism and the complete removal of the socialist threat, men and women on the make can see no pressing or urgent cause to dedicate their lives to the public service. The bourgeoisie no longer have anything to fear. So what possible bourgeois incentive might there be to desert the counting house for Westminster, still less for the city hall or the village hall. Nothing in it for them. Quite simply, from a bourgeois point of view, an authoritative and charismatic political class has been rendered superfluous, or even – if it were to start wanting to interfere with market forces, or to put an end to gutter journalism and barrow-boy finance, soft porn TV, and all the other evils of our time – potentially dangerous. The last thing a triumphant bourgeoisie wants is the smack of firm government, preferring instead to put their faith in Adam Smith's 'invisible hand'. Nor is it only the bourgeois high-flyers who take this view. So do Mr and Mrs Average Briton. For while the former has deserted Westminster for the City, the latter has deserted the polling booth for the shopping mall. While in the case of the former it is the satisfaction of making money as an entrepreneur that has seduced them away from politics, in the case of the latter it is the satisfaction of spending money as a consumer. We have not so much a Britain made safe for democracy as one made so safe as to be able to do without democracy, or at any rate without democrats, if by democrats are meant citizens who care actively and self-sacrificingly about the common weal.

Unfortunately, making even more strenuous efforts to maximize upward social mobility will only make matters worse because most of the beneficiaries will only want to join the very economic class that prefers a weak political class: a political class it can put on its payroll. So while many ambitious individuals will gain from an easier ascent, society as a whole will suffer. The old political class that used to give the lead in every walk of life will remain in the wings and no new authoritative political class will emerge to take its place. Politicians will go on thinking up wondrous new plans and projects to improve the nation's lot but, because the relationship between those who give the orders and those who receive them, at least in the public sector, has become so chaotically disordered, nothing will work. The old rules will no longer apply but without an authoritative political class to draw up new ones, everybody will feel free to make their own. This may be a recipe for maximizing the pursuit of individual happiness, but it most emphatically is not a recipe for the good government of a nation wanting to make its mark on the world. The results are all around us: in the hospitals, on the railways, on the streets, in the classroom; everywhere, except in the armed forces or on the rugby field, the two areas where the old values, rather than the invisible hand, are still in charge.

In short, Britain is beginning to miss the existence of a political class that saw it as its duty to give a lead, which, of course, is precisely what the old political class, adhering to aristocratic values, most famously did and, I believe, could do again if encouraged rather than discouraged to do so. Shorn of its old statutory privileges, of course; but also shorn of its current anti-aristocratic handicaps. No more demands, for example, to keep public-school candidates out of Oxbridge colleges on egalitarian principle, in spite of their proven ability to win places there in open and competitive examinations.

Here, however, we run head-on into the problem of Britain's two-tier educational system. So long as that remains, so long will be there be justification for believing in the continued existence of Lord Snooty, in spite of his ejection from the House of Lords. Although Eton has long since stopped producing such obnoxious specimens, today's old Etonians are – against all reason – still associated with this much mocked stereotype, which is why constituency associations, Civil Service boards, and pretty well all the other national institutions shy away from them as if they were some kind of exotic, poisoned fruit.* So a further conclusive *coup de grâce* may be necessary to put the egalitarians out of business.

While pondering on what this might be, memory took me back to those conversations with that aforementioned *rentier* uncle of mine, R. C. Norman† who showed such *grand* wisdom in disarming Old Labour's egalitarian offensives after its election triumph some sixty years ago. Essentially his strategy was for Old England to make its traditions and habits of authority available – not to say indispensable – to the smooth operation of the welfare state, to the point where true-blue Toryism became almost as much an organic part of the New Jerusalem as Old Labour's socialism. What comparably statesmanlike service would Ronnie Norman have Old Britain provide today?

Something, I believe, along the following lines: that the Provost of Eton – needless to say RCN was an Old Etonian – with the backing of all the governors of the other great public schools, should take the initiative in bringing to an end the poisonous divide in our system of education – good schools for the rich and pretty, poor ones, in general, for the poor. Acting as spokesman for all these historic institutions, the Provost would propose that they form the catalyst for a new tier in the state sector of education specifically

---

* Or if they are accepted, they are required to disguise themselves out of all recognition.
† See p. 38.

aimed at producing a cultivated and civilized political class, not unlike the role played in France by *les grandes écoles*. His reason for making this dramatic proposal, the Provost would explain, was that, under market pressure, and to his great regret, the public schools were being forced to abandon their traditional role. Instead of concentrating on producing future statesmen, ambassadors, generals, judges, governors of the Bank of England, and so on and such like, they were now reduced to producing supremely self-confident wheeler-dealers more than a match in sharp practice, skulduggery, and predator instinct for any East End barrow boy. Old Etonian charm and elegance, he would concede, are still to be found in abundance. But whereas those weapons used to be put to public benefit, they are now put to private gain. It was a deplorable state of affairs. No sooner did an Old Etonian leave the school than his one preoccupation was to convince a prospective employer, probably in the City, that his four years there had not left him in any way tainted by the humane and gentlemanly values such an education was once intended to instil. In other words, in their primary role of replenishing the ranks of the political and administrative class, the public schools are now more a minus than a plus.

The trouble was, the Provost would continue, that all the most glittering prizes were now to be found in the realms of private enterprise. Left to the mercy of the market these pressures could only get worse. Were the public schools to encourage their best pupils to go into parliament or, worse, local government – as they would like to do –

parents might well ask for their money back. The public schools were in a no-win situation. Of course this was not true of all parents: some simply wanted their children to be well educated. But not many, because being well educated in any true sense today could prove a horrible handicap, inculcating scruples, virtues, sensitivities, finer feelings, none of which were of much help in 'the real world'.

For these reasons, the Provost would go on to say, he had come to the conclusion that the public schools might be better off – assuming they could negotiate the right conditions – in the state system; better off in the sense of being more able, once freed from the pressures of the market, to revert to their Victorian function of producing a public-spirited and civilized political class. In the old days, with the State threatening to nationalize the public schools by diktat, such an offer would have been out of the question. But on this occasion the proposal, he would emphasize, was coming from the public schools themselves. It was they who were voluntarily, *and in the public interest*, offering to make the public-school mould available to suitably qualified and motivated children from all classes in a new education sector publicly financed on the same kind of national interest grounds as were the BBC, the National Gallery, and the British Museum.

Finally, as a parting shot, the Provost would go on to say that the public schools were taking a great risk in making such an offer. Many of the rich parents whose children would not qualify under the new arrangements would be up in arms. But once the penny dropped that a public-school education was not a passport to the best posts in private enterprise, but rather a passport to relatively low-paid jobs in the public service – in politics, in the churches, in the armed forces, even in the social services – he was sure their anger would soon evaporate, and then, *faute de mieux*, most of these same parents might start to turn their attention and use their immense energies and influence towards making the main state system better – to the lasting benefit of the nation as a whole. In conclusion, what he was proposing was nothing less than a long overdue revolution in British education; a revolution, moreover, as acceptable *in principle*, to the Left as to the Right: a one-nation solution owing nothing to New Labour or to the New Conservatives and everything to the dramatic emergence in the first decade of the twenty-first century of the good old aristocratic notion of *noblesse oblige*.

Yes, I am dreaming. In the present climate, the public schools are not going to make any such proposal. An act of creative statesmanship of this order, which might set the public's imagination racing and make politics seem a noble endeavour again, is less and less imaginable as Britain becomes more and more classless. Which brings me, in conclusion, to the point of writing this essay. Its whole purpose has been to try to engender a change in this climate; to try to show how essential it is to reactivate the aristocratic leaven. With that leaven a bourgeois society can make *progress*, even reach for the stars; without it, there will be no alternative but to stick in the mud. Of course, ideally, it should be a small boy who points out that the classless society emperor has no clothes. Unfortunately I am not a small boy; only an octogenarian quite probably in his second childhood, which, come to think of it, may be the next best thing.

Index

Abingdon, 12th Earl of 16
Acheson, Dean 135, 136, 167n
Adams, John 148
Adonis, Andrew 201
Africa 115, 183
Ainsworth, Harrison 36
Aldrich, Nelson W. 51n
Algeria 179
Alsop, Joseph W. 124n, 135n, 136, 137–8
Alsop, Stewart 136
American Civil War 112
American Revolution (1776) 121
Amis, Kingsley 93
Ancram, Earl of 215
Annan, Noel 23
Arnold, Matthew 13n, 41–2, 80, 214
Arundel Castle 17
Asia 183
Astor family 16
Athens 14
Attlee, Clement 195, 199
Auchincloss, Louis 142
Auden, W.H. 29
Ayer, Freddie 145n

Bacon, Francis 112
Baldwin, James 156–7
Baldwin, Stanley 17, 25–30, 32, 104
Baltzell, E. Digby 124n, 142
Bank of England 17, 18, 33, 34, 45, 223
Barnett, Correlli 195

BBC (British Broadcasting Corporation) 35, 38, 107, 156, 224
BBC Two 217
Beaconsfield, Bucks 13
Beaverbrook, Max Aitken, Lord 28n, 34
Beer, Samuel 101
Benn, Tony 191
Bevan, Aneurin 56–8, 76, 193n, 197
Beveridge, William 152
Bevin, Ernest 51n, 136
Birnbaum, Pierre 168n, 170n, 180–81
Bismarck, Prince Otto von 195
Black family 35
Blair, Tony 2, 103, 215n
Blake, Robert 143n
Boethius, Anicius 20
Bolshevik Party 67
Boone, Daniel 124
Boothby, Robert, Lord 32
Boston, Massachusetts 118, 127, 140
British Empire 114, 137, 148
British Museum, London 54, 224
Brooks, David 162–6
Buchan, John 137, 206
Bundy, Harvey 167n
Bundy, William 167n
Burckhardt, Jacob 61
Burke, Edmund 13–14, 43, 78, 81, 114, 165
Burnley, Lancashire 36, 38

227

Burnley Corporation 36
Burroughs, William S. 162
Burton, Robert 20
Bush, George W. 164n
Bush family 109, 110
Butterfield, Herbert 55–6, 60, 68
Byron, George Gordon, Lord 54

Cabinet Office 40
Café Royal, Regent Street, London 58
Cambridge University 45, 60n, 82, 127
Cannadine, David 114, 208, 211–12
Canning, George 58
Carnegie, Andrew 154
Catholicism, Catholics 16, 17, 25, 128, 134, 171, 175–82, 188, 192, 202, 212
Cavendish, Henry 54
Cecil, Lord David 143–4
Census Bureau (US) 131
Central African Federation 115
Chamberlain, Neville 18, 25, 30, 32
Chamberlain family 141–2
Channon, Chips 25, 33
Charles I, King 67
Charleston 118
Chartists 85
Chatham, William Pitt, 1st Earl of 58
Chevallier, Michel 111–12
Chicago 125
Chirac, Jacques 186
Church of England 65, 84, 87, 89, 99
Churchill, Jack 37
Churchill, Sir Winston 11, 30, 31, 32, 37, 134, 194
City of London 33, 40, 87, 220, 223
Civil Service 12, 87, 190, 221
Clark, Jonathan 202–3, 204
Clemenceau, Georges 176

Clinton, Bill 164n
Cliviger Gorge 36, 37
Cobden, Richard 54
Colasse, Claude Bertrand de 168
Cold War 90, 127, 152
Collini, Stefan 51n
Conant, Dr James B. 147–8, 150–55
Connaught Grill, Mayfair, London 46
Conservative government 91
Conservative Party 6n, 89, 103, 104–5, 107, 195, 196, 198
Cooper, Alfred Duff, 1st Viscount Norwich 32
'Correspondent' programme 217
Covent Garden Opera House 106
Crosland, Anthony 160–61
Cuban Missile Crisis 144, 145, 167n
Cumberland Lodge, Windsor Park 17
Curley, Mayor 127
Curzon of Kedleston, Marquis 136

Daily Telegraph 167n
Davenport, John 19–20
David, Jacques-Louis 170n
Davies, Sir Dan 76n
Dawson, Geoffrey 45–6
Day, Sir Robin 59
Declaration of Independence 124, 148
Democratic Party (US) 138
Depression 89, 134, 135, 140, 145
Descartes, René 112
Devonshire, Duke of 143
Dibelius, Dr 82
Disraeli, Benjamin 2, 58
Douglas-Home, Charles 208
Dyneley 37

East India Company 81
École nationale d'administration (ENA) 178, 180, 182, 185, 186, 187

Edward VII, King (as Prince of Wales) 114
Edward VIII, King (later Duke of Windsor) 25, 26
Eisenhower, Dwight D. 138–9
Eliot, T.S. 5n, 41
Elizabeth II, Queen 212
Emerson, Edward 126
Emerson, Ralph Waldo 126, 151
Engels, Friedrich 68
English Civil War 65
Enlightenment 113–14, 115, 172, 175, 202, 217
Eton College 16, 17, 22–3, 33, 145n, 197, 200–201, 221–2

Fifth Republic (France) 180, 182, 185n
First World War 25, 26, 176
Fisher, Sir Warren 35
Fitzalan, Edmund 16, 17, 25
Flaubert, Gustave 80
Ford, Henry 81
Foreign Office 136
Fortescue, Sir John 168
Fourth Republic (France) 90, 177–9
Fox, Charles James 58, 85
Franco-French civil war 175, 177
Frankfurter, Felix 137
French Revolution 24, 97, 121, 169–71, 192, 199, 202

Gaitskell, Hugh 2
Gates, Bill 163
Gaulle, Charles de 55, 168, 178–81, 183, 185–6
Gaullism 193
General Strike (1926) 32n, 76, 104
George V, King 17
George VI, King 76n
Gerrards Cross, Bucks 13
Gestapo 194
Gladstone, William Ewart 2, 58
Glorious Revolution (1688) 67, 70, 71, 121

Goonie, Lady 37
Gooreynd, Alexander Koch de 15–16
Grainger, J.H. 88n
grand bourgeois 2
Grenadier Guards 193

Hacker, Andrew 157, 158–9, 160
Haffner, Sebastian 32n
Harriman, Averill 135
Hartington, Marquis of 54, 143
Harvard University 127, 136, 147, 149, 150, 152
Hastings, Warren 81
Hayek, Professor F.A. 194n
Henderson, Nicko 23
Himmelfarb, Gertrude 58n, 156
Hirsch, Baron 130
Hitler, Adolf 17, 30, 31, 32n
Hobbes, Thomas 72
Hofstadter, Richard 90–91
Hoggart, Richard 10, 11
Hollis, Christopher 30
Holmes, Oliver Wendell 19, 126
Hopkins, Sir Richard 35
House of Commons 57, 59, 70, 194, 214
House of Lords 3, 5, 59, 65, 67, 87, 89, 94, 96, 103, 105, 122, 128, 201, 208, 214, 215, 218, 221
House Un-American Activities Committee 136
Howard, Anthony 217n
Howard, Michael 2
Hurd, Douglas 106n

Industrial Revolution 12, 47
Irish Guards 16, 17

Jackson, Andrew 119
Jackson, Julian 174n
Jacksonian revolution 102
Jacobins 74, 77, 121
Jacobites 68, 69
James, Henry 125–6, 157, 167

James, William 125–6
Jefferson, Thomas 118, 122,
    148–9, 153
Jenkins, Roy, Lord 93, 98
Jesus Christ 77
Jowett, Dr 148

Kalakaua, King of Hawaii 114
Kee, Robert 21n, 23
Kemsley, Lord and Lady 34–5
Kennan, George 136
Kennedy, Jackie (later Onassis)
    142, 143
Kennedy, John F. 52–3, 126–7,
    140, 142–7, 167n
Kennedy, Joseph P. 126, 141, 142,
    143
Kennedy, Robert 140
Kennedy family 109–10, 142, 143,
    144
Kerry, John F. 167n
Keynes, John Maynard 17, 27
King's College, Cambridge 33
Kristol, Irving 156
Krugman, Paul R. 110
Krupp, Alfred 28n

La Guardia, Mayor 127
Labour government 133, 195, 214
Labour Party 28, 60, 80, 87, 135,
    193, 196, 214, 216
Laski, Harold J. 54–5, 89, 90
Lee, Jenny, Baroness 76
Lemann, Nicholas 150n
Leopold, King of the Belgians 36
Letwin, Oliver 201n
Letwin, Shirley 201n
Lincoln, Abraham 124–5, 135
Lincoln, Robert Todd 125
Lippmann, Walter 18, 137
Lloyd George, David 88
London County Council 35
Louis XIV, King of France (the
    Sun King) 71, 116, 169, 171,
    172, 173, 180, 183

Lovett, Bob 135
Lukacs, John 1–2, 129n
Luther, Martin 112

Macaulay, Thomas Babington, lst
    Baron 54
McCarthy, Joe 138–9, 140
McCarthyism 90, 139, 140
McCloy, John 135–6
McElwee, Bill 23
Macmillan, Harold, 1st Earl of
    Stockton 2, 91, 114–15
Maine 132, 137
Maistre, Joseph de 175, 177
Major, John 93
Mallock, W.H. 58
Mandelstam, Nadezhda 81
Mann, Thomas 2, 141
Mao Zedong 12, 15
Maritain, Jacques 182
Marshall, Arthur 102
Marshall Aid 195
Marx, Karl 27, 68
Mary, Queen 17
Mason, Philip 191n
Maurras, Charles 175, 177
MCC (Marylebone Cricket Club) 87
Melbourne, Lord 143
Members of Parliament (MPs)
    95–6, 98–9
Menand, Louis 19, 126
Mental Health Association 36
Metropolitan Club, New York 137
Mexico 132
MI5 127
MI6 127
Mill, John Stuart 3, 101
Milner, Lord 137
miners' strike 104
Mitterrand, François 186
Montaigne 182, 187
Moore, Henry 39
More Place, Hertfordshire 197
Morris, Jan 125
Mosca, Gaetano 107–8

Mosley, Sir Oswald 89–90
Murdoch, Rupert 208
Murdoch family 35

Naipaul, V.S. 93, 214
Namier, Sir Lewis 59
Napoleon Bonaparte 142, 146, 171, 172
Napoleonic Wars 104
National Gallery, London 224
National Health Service 197
National Trust 51
New Conservative Party/ Conservatives 48, 58, 102, 104, 105–6, 225
New Deal 26, 132, 145
New Labour/Labourites 48, 58, 102, 105, 107, 225
New York 118, 125, 156
Newman, Cardinal 79
Nietzsche, Friedrich 41
Nigeria, Northern 115
Nitze, Paul 135
Nixon, Richard 143n
Norfolk, Duke of 16
Norman, Montagu 17, 25, 28, 30–36, 38, 39, 132, 194, 199
Norman, R.C. 38–9, 194–8, 222
Norman family 25, 39, 40
Northcliffe, Lord 16

Oakeshott, Michael 60–61, 63, 74
Office of Strategic Studies 127
Old Etonians 196, 201n, 222, 223
Old Labour 87, 90, 98–102, 222
Old Stoics 23
Old Tories 15, 102
Ortega y Gasset, José 7n
Orwell, George 86
Oxbridge 12, 87, 106, 200, 206–8, 216, 221
Oxford University 82, 105, 127

Palmerston, Lord 58
Paris 77, 180, 181, 185

Paxman, Jeremy 59
Peel, Sir Robert 2
Pétain, Marshal 176
Philadelphia 118, 127, 133
Pilgrim Fathers 116
Pitt, William, the Younger 85
Plato 13
Pollock, Frederick 126
Pompidou, Georges 185n
Pratt's Club, St James's, London 46
Proust, Marcel 2
Prussia 195

Quinton, Tony 23

Radziwill, Prince 143
Reading, Lady 36
Reformation 64, 112
Reith, Sir John 17, 35
Remington, Frederick 129, 131
Republican Party (US) 138
Reputations (TV programme) 58
Reyntiens, Lady Alice 36–8
Reyntiens, Major Robert 36
Robespierre, Maximilien 187
Rockefeller family 109–10
Rolling Stones 162
Roosevelt, Eleanor 133, 145
Roosevelt, Franklin D. 26, 132, 133, 134, 137, 145
Roosevelt, Theodore 129
Root, Jane 217
Rose, Jonathan 57
Rothermere, Harold Harmsworth, Lord 28n
Rousseau, Jean-Jacques 113
Rowse, A.L. 51
Roxburgh, J.F. 22–3
Royal Navy 83
Russell, Lord John 54
Russia/Russians 67, 145, 179, 188
Russian Revolution 97

Salisbury, Lord 2, 36
Scargill, Arthur 104

Schacht, Dr 17, 30
Schumpeter, Joseph 14, 43
Second World War 31, 34, 45, 90, 91, 134, 145, 147, 176–7
Secret, M. 187
Shaftesbury, Lord 54
Shakespeare, William 51
Shils, Professor Edward 73, 156
Shriver, Sargent 142
Siedentop, Larry 187n
Sinatra, Frank 142
Skidelsky, Edward 217n
Smith, Adam 88
Snow, C.P. 52
Social Register 125
Sokoto, Sarduana of 115
Solzhenitsyn, Alexander 179
Soviet Union 29n, 199
Spencer, Lady 114
Stowe School 20, 21–3
Stuart, Charles Edward (Young Pretender) 69
Stuarts 64, 69
student revolt (France, 1968) 185
Switzerland 62, 214

Taft, Robert 138
Taft, William Howard 138
Taine, Hippolyte A. 74
Terror (France) 77
Thatcher, Margaret, Baroness 103–4, 106n
Third Republic (France) 172–6, 178, 180, 182, 196
Thomas, Jimmy 133
Thornton, A.P. 69
Thyssen, Fritz 28n
Times, The 16, 44–5, 135, 136, 207–8
Tocqueville, Alexis de 9, 24–5, 48, 54, 74, 85–6, 96, 109, 116, 117, 118, 119, 121, 122, 152, 160
Today programme 166
Tomalin, Claire 77n

Tories 69, 128, 193n, 216
Towneley family 36, 37
Towneley Hall 36–7
Treasury 35
Trevelyan, Sir Charles 51
Trevelyan, G.M. 39, 51
Truman, Harry S. 135

US Marine Corps 145

Vichy regime 176, 177, 178
Victoria, Queen 143, 201
Vietnam War 167n
Voltaire 74, 175

Walden, George 52n
Wallington, Northumberland 51
War Office 40
Washington, George 141, 147
Washington DC 125, 127, 135, 137, 152, 165
Waugh, Evelyn 25, 51, 52n, 125
Weber, Max 38, 109, 187n
Welensky, Roy 115
Wellington, Arthur Wellesley, 1st Duke of 87, 146
Welsh Guards 145n
Westminster, Duke of 208–12
Westminster Estate, London 209
Whigs 58, 69, 143, 144
Wilhelm II, Kaiser (as Crown Prince) 114
Williamson, Philip 26n
Wilson, Edmund 81
Wister, Owen 129–30, 131
Wodehouse, P.G. 90n
Wolin, Professor Sheldon 111, 119
Wollstonecraft, Mary 77
Women's Voluntary Service (WVS later WRVS) 36
Worsthorne, Lancashire 16n
Wyatt, Woodrow 76n

Yale University 127, 167ni